# REIKI

# REIKI

The art of healing through
universal energy

CARMEN FERNANDEZ

LORENZ BOOKS

# Contents

# Introduction

Reiki, a Japanese word pronounced ray-key, can be translated to mean universal life force, or universally guided energy. It is a very simple system of healing, carried out by placing hands on or over a person (who is always clothed), or animal or plant, with the intent to channel Reiki. It can also be sent, as absent healing, over distance and even through time.

Reiki, thought to have been practised for thousands of years, was rediscovered in the 19th century by Dr Mikao Usui of Japan. Dr Usui made his findings after researching ancient Buddhist documents on the power of healing. Following these revelations, Dr Usui then proceeded to share the secrets of Reiki with others. These secrets have been passed down from master to student, and were introduced to the West during the 1960s and 1970s. Now there are thousands of Reiki teachers and practitioners, as the message spreads that Reiki can be practised by anyone following attunements given by a master.

Reiki heals on all levels, physically, mentally and spiritually, and supports the body's natural ability to heal itself. The characteristic heat of Reiki can often be physically felt without actual touch. Reiki is a non-confrontational form of healing, soothing away many different troubles and traumas in a very gentle way. It is also non-denominational, practised by people of many different religions and cultures. You don't need to commit to a belief system in order to channel Reiki, or enjoy its benefits; all you need is the desire to heal and be healed.

This book serves as a valuable introduction to all aspects of Reiki for those who aspire to feel its healing energy and universal love, and to inspire those who already enjoy the balancing effects of this all-embracing, healing art.

# Universal Life Force

All the universe has come from love,

and to love all things return.

For from joy all beings have come,

by joy they all live,

and unto joy they all return.

THE TAITTIRIYA UPANISHAD

# Reiki is love

To experience Reiki is to experience the communication of love from the Universe to all beings. Instinctively tactile, we know from birth the joy that comes from the loving touch of another person.

The sensation of touch is present in many of the wonderful healing arts available to us, and we feel the comfort of a person's touch before their healing skills benefit our bodies and uplift our spirits. To receive Reiki, through your own hands or those of another person, is to be held and supported by the life force of the Universe itself. It is to receive cosmic energy which flows through everything on the Earth.

Below: The effect of Reiki is similar to the sun shining on the earth, and we should remember this when we enjoy the intense heat of the sun on our bodies, in the same way as Dr Usui carried a bright lantern in order to remind himself of Reiki's intense healing energy.

*There is a light that shines beyond all things on earth, beyond us all, beyond the heavens, beyond the highest, the very highest heavens. This is the light that shines in our heart.*
THE CHANDOGYA UPANISHAD

## Communication and the cosmos

The origin of Reiki is the same loving Universe that gives us breath each second. Reiki invites us to open up to this great love, trusting it and allowing it to flow through us. "Rei" can be translated as universal, or spiritually guided; "ki" is the energy or life force present in everything. Reiki is literally energy (ki) guided by divine wisdom (rei).

Having its own intelligence, Reiki has no boundaries, yet it knows where it is most welcome. The energy that passes through a Reiki practitioner's palms is impossible to hold on to because it belongs to everyone and everything, and no-one can harness it – it is intangible.

In the modern world Reiki flourishes everywhere, and for the many who are able to enjoy it, it is a wonderful physical, emotional and spiritual healing which blesses all it reaches. Reiki brings us comfort from pain, creativity when we feel stifled, and love when we feel separate.

Above: Essential energy of the Universe, Reiki is infinite in flow, past and future, and unfettered by concepts of time and space.

## Reiki is for everyone

Whether your life seems lacking or you live it to the full, whether you are a spiritual seeker, a single-minded materialist, experiencing a period of depression or adapting to change, Reiki embraces and enriches everyone. The energy which permeates the Cosmos is divine wisdom and truth. It transcends time and space, and all religions. It is enjoyed by people of many faiths and of no faith, and promotes positive living and compassion for all.

## Universal law

In many different ways, Reiki shows us the happiness we can feel by living in harmony with the laws of the Universe. Love, if you want to be loved; give willingly and you will receive many times. The person channelling Reiki is never drained, as the energy reaches the healer before it reaches the person being healed. We are eternally replenished, which shows us that there is enough of everything to go round. Reiki has been found to be a non-polar energy – it has no opposite. It can only be used to bring good, and if, in a moment of weakness, we attempt to use Reiki to manipulate an outcome which is not for the highest good, it simply does not work.

## Giving and receiving Reiki

Many people feel a conscious connection to all life forming in their hearts following their Reiki attunement. You need no intellectual skills to use Reiki, or to receive it – only an open mind and the intent to heal. Following a Reiki attunement, the ability to channel the power of Reiki is instant and everlasting. Reiki is unconditional love in a world often beset by conflict, and it begins with you.

# The Story of Reiki

No-one knows for certain when Reiki was first channelled to heal self and others. Some Reiki practitioners feel that Reiki was known and used for spiritual benefit in the legendary civilizations of Lemuria and Atlantis, while others suggest that Reiki has been the loving energy behind many kinds of healing miracles throughout the ages.

## The rediscovery of reiki

The story of how Dr Mikao Usui rediscovered Reiki was originally passed down in oral tradition. Each Reiki master/teacher still relates in turn the story they have been taught. It is due to this oral tradition that there are variations in the story of Reiki, but it does not matter if we do not know the exact details of Dr Usui's quest for Reiki or the exact circumstances in which Reiki reappeared to the world. Reiki's story has symbolic value – above all, it tells of a quest from the heart and that is always relevant.

Mikao Usui was born on 15 August 1862, in southern Japan. Although he never received formal training as an allopathic doctor, he was bestowed with this title in his lifetime, in recognition of his commitment to heal wherever he saw suffering. He has been depicted as both a practising Buddhist and a devout Christian; alterations may have been made to suit the politics of the day, or perhaps this illustrates his universal and all-embracing approach to sharing the gift he found with those in need of love everywhere. The story told by my Reiki master says that it was while teaching at a school in Kyoto that Dr Usui was first prompted to seek a method of healing through touch. His young students had been taught the scriptures and had heard with fascination Jesus's words, "You will do as I have done and even greater things." The students asked why ordinary people could not heal through touch and if the legacy left by great healers was the message that everyone could heal if they truly sought the answers. Dr Usui's quest began.

## In search of a formula

In order to find answers, Dr Usui began years of study in monasteries and libraries in the United States, China, India and Tibet. He learned Sanskrit and read the Buddhist teachings in the ancient sutras, or spiritual texts. During this time many wonderful blessings were revealed to Dr Usui, but he wanted to be able to put his new knowledge into practice. All the secrets revealed to him were experienced in an intellectual sense, and Dr Usui knew he must translate what he had learned into action if it was to heal. Yearning to discover a physical formula, he decided he would meditate on his desire to do this, and travelled to sacred Mount Koriyama in northern Japan.

## The 21 stones

On reaching Mount Koriyama, Dr Usui gathered 21 stones and made a pile, intending to throw one stone away at the end of each day. The number 21 is quite significant here, and occurs in the ancient writings of many religions. During this time, he contemplated all he had learned, read and experienced, and meditated on the symbols he had seen in the scriptures. Dr Usui had still not found his answers when the first light of the 21st day began to dawn. As he stood on the mountain looking into the dark sky, he could see a light hurtling straight towards him. He did not move, and the ball of light grew and grew until it finally hit him between the eyes. Dr Usui was convinced he was about to die when he saw millions of tiny bubbles in every colour of the rainbow. The symbols and the very essence of their meanings were contained within the

Above: Reiki is the essential energy of the Universe, and it was while he was meditating on the mountain that Dr Usui was blessed with the knowledge of Reiki.

bubbles, and Dr Usui immediately understood them. He said, "I remember." The answers to his prayers had landed on his sixth chakra, the seat of insight and intuition. On his way down the mountain Dr Usui stubbed his toe. Instinctively, he placed his hands over the wound, to relieve his injury. When he removed them, the bleeding had stopped and the toe was healed. It was the first of his Reiki miracles.

## Into the world

Dr Usui decided to take the gift of Reiki to the places where it was needed most. The slums of Kyoto became his clinic for several years, and the healing power of Reiki was very successful at treating many physical disorders. He began to realize he could attune others to heal them-selves, and began a new life travelling and teaching, and healing with Reiki. He is buried in Kyoto cemetery, where the beautiful inscription on his gravestone is a testament to his deep commitment to and love for all living things.

## The first grand masters

One of Dr Usui's greatest friends was a young man named Chijiro Hayashi, a naval officer. Dr Usui passed on the lineage of Reiki to Hayashi, who became the Second Grand Master and who formed the three degrees of Reiki. The third Grand Master Mr Hayashi ran a Reiki clinic in Tokyo. Mrs Hawayo Takata, ill from cancer, received Reiki healing, and after her recovery she persuaded Hayashi to accept her as a pupil. She studied with him for a year, after which she returned to her birthplace of Hawaii, where she was later made Grand Master, the 13th and last Reiki master who had been personally attuned by Mr Hayashi.

# Reiki ethics

The ethics of living in the spirit of Reiki were formed by Dr Usui after working in the slums of Kyoto, which taught him much about human nature and the world around him, and which lay the foundation for the five principles.

The five principles are really a guide to living with a happy heart, whatever your path in life, and promoting harmony with the world around you, and they can be considered a healing treatment in themselves. Today, there are many variations on the five Reiki principles, so you can

find one which "speaks" to you. The following version was laid down by Hawayo Takata. Dwell on and in them, and allow them to filter through your consciousness.

## Just for today do not worry

If, each morning, you choose to wake up trusting that whatever the day brings will be a valuable and wonderful experience, you are living this principle. Worry can take up much of our lives – if we are not worrying over past mistakes, we are often fearing the future. We are brought up to compete and to struggle, and this breeds in us an inherent lack of trust in the world around us. We can see the big picture much more clearly when we place our trust in the Divine Plan.

## Just for today do not anger

Anger can be transformative, and we do not need to hang on to it if we learn that it has such a positive use. What are we angry about? Maybe we feel trapped by a situation or a person. We may fear harmful results for ourselves and others. Recognize how you feel, acknowledge that we are all learning together, and know that all is well. The ability to stand back from our own feelings is empowering. Anger can be a destructive force, but analyzing it can be a catalyst for positive change.

## Honour your elders and teachers

Everyone can teach us something. Parents, elders and children too, if we listen. If you

Left: Greet the day with a salute to the sun; adding ritual to your morning routine will create a happy day.

decide to become a teacher of Reiki you will soon discover how important and enriching it is to bless and thank your students for what they, in turn, teach you. This principle is also helpful in recognizing the value of being non-judgemental in life. Whatever someone's path, it is theirs and as valid as your own. Acknowledge and respect this and create freedom for yourself and others.

## Earn your living honestly

So many ethical questions abound in the world of work today that living with integrity is important if we are to be at peace with ourselves and our own truth. No matter how small the job, it is our present moment nonetheless, and if we put our hearts into it and do it with love, we will be giving and getting the most from that moment. This principle can also inspire us to have the courage to find work in a field we truly love, fulfilling our purpose.

## Show gratitude to everything

Our personal beliefs, and the thoughts and emotions they breed, are the most important contributing factor to our state of health. We have all experienced the benefits of positive thinking in our lives, and how it helps us to be happier. Research shows that recovery from illness, and immunity from disease, is strongest among people who love themselves, others and

Above: Enjoying the beauty of life is at the heart of Reiki – take time to appreciate nature's gifts and use your senses to the full.

# The Spiritual Principles

Just for today do not worry

Just for today do not anger

Honour your parents, teachers and elders

Earn your living honestly

Show gratitude to everything

life, and who use techniques like visualization. Positivity and the expression of love are as powerful as diet in the treatment of disease. It is a thrilling revelation to discover how an attitude of gratitude enhances life – and how swiftly. The moment we wake up feeling "thank you" instead of "please", the universe begins to echo our positive new thought patterns – and send some more of it our way. The last of the five Reiki principles, this goes a long way towards living all of them, and creating our own reality. Bless your life and it will be even more joyful.

# Reiki schools – the many in the one

There may be as many as 30 different variations of Reiki being practised in the world today. These branches of Reiki all descend from, or are linked to, the original Usui System of Natural Healing.

The human mind is great at separating, and there is some argument today as to what is traditional and what is accepted in the Reiki world. Included here are brief descriptions and explanations of the origins of some of the many Reiki schools thriving today. Follow your heart and you will find what you are looking for.

*There is nothing on earth so curious for beauty or so absorbent of it as a soul.*
WASSILY KANDINSKY

## Rainbow reiki

Rainbow Reiki was initially developed as a healing system by Walter Lubeck and, as the name suggests, Rainbow practitioners use many tools with which to empower and complement the Usui system. Crystals are often used for healing purposes and can be powerfully complemented with a Reiki energy charge. Rainbow Reiki aims to put us in touch with our Inner Child, and is a fruitful and enjoyable way

Below: Rainbow Reiki is a powerful healer. It can be used to reconnect us with our inner child, who still knows our dreams and aspirations even when the logical mind feels out of touch.

to rediscover untapped creativity, happiness and a clear perception of where we are in our lives. Its practices include the unique Powerball Technique as well as aspects of shamanism.

## Karuna reiki

Karuna Reiki is often described as the Reiki of Compassionate Action. It was developed by William Lee Rand, and is considered among Karuna practitioners to be the next step on from Usui Reiki, with Karuna attunements available only to Reiki practitioners who have already attained master/teacher level. Karuna is a Sanskrit word meaning "a compassionate action intended to relieve suffering from all sentient beings". A total of 12 Karuna Reiki symbols are taught at two levels of proficiency, each symbol possessing a precise energy and used for healing at deep, cellular levels.

## Seichem reiki

Seichem Reiki is said to have its roots in the same sutras in which Usui was given the traditional Reiki symbols. Seichem

Above: Hands-on healing in association with powerful symbols has been part of the spiritual knowledge of Tibet for thousands of years.

Below: With the faith that we can assist our own healing, we create a revolution in our minds, changing our pattern of consciousness.

practitioners claim that not all the information of Reiki is passed on within the Usui system. Apparently, an Usui master and a Seichem master met and exchanged their information and ideas. Seichem was found to have two additional symbols, used to profound healing effect. Dr Usui is said to have attuned many people during his lifetime, and Seichem was one of many schools which later grew from his teachings. Seichem works in harmony with the elements of earth, air, fire and water, as well as ether, which connects to the higher realms of existence.

## Tibetan reiki

Tibetan Reiki is sometimes taught in conjunction with Usui Reiki, and is often said to be the closest to it. Some of the symbols used are very similar to the symbols used in Usui Reiki, with almost identical pronunciation. They are also possibly of shamanic origin, like many symbols from the ancient world still used today.

# Having a healing

What might prompt your first experience of receiving Reiki and searching for a practitioner? Perhaps you are in physical pain or discomfort. Perhaps you are feeling under pressure and are looking for a soothing relaxation method. You might want to complement other therapeutic skills which you have already tried.

Maybe you are just curious to know more about this all-round healing phenomenon, or maybe you feel this is the right channel for your own healing powers. All of these reasons could spur you to seek out a Reiki practitioner, whether online, through new age magazines, or by word of mouth, and often it seems that Reiki finds you once you are interested.

### Finding a tailor-made service

What are you looking for in a Reiki practitioner? Some of us are happy to make an appointment and to turn up on the day, others may have

Above: Purples and blues and dreamy images are commonly seen by the person receiving Reiki, as their whole being opens in response to the loving energy.

Below: On the first meeting a Reiki practitioner may give you a questionnaire to fill in, or you might have a chat about your general health and wellbeing.

special considerations to take into account. Although Reiki is strictly a clothes-on, hands-on affair, you may want to choose a Reiki practitioner with whom you feel comfortable and gender may be a part of this issue. If you are not mobile, you may be looking for a practitioner who is; many carry portable couches and will visit your home, in which case will there be noisy children running about when you need peace and quiet? Alternatively, they may practise from theirs. Available times must be arranged, of course, and you may want to know the duration of the Reiki session, usually about an hour. Make enquiries about charges – rates vary widely, and many practitioners offer concessions or are willing to make an exchange for special skills or services.

## The reiki experience

Your Reiki practitioner will probably want to know a little bit about your general health and your lifestyle before he or she begins. They will ask you to take off your shoes for comfort, and perhaps any metal jewellery in case it interrupts the Reiki flow or prevents your free movement. Even if you have a specific injury, you will receive a full-body treatment working from head to toe with the traditional hand positions. However, if your body won't allow free access, don't worry – the Reiki will get there anyway.

The practitioner will usually remain quiet during the session; this is because it is your time, to relax and to let the gentle power of Reiki flow into your being. However, as you relax you may want to ask questions, or express yourself, or even to laugh or cry or giggle – there is no right or wrong reaction to Reiki. It simply facilitates holistic healing and promotes wellbeing in a gentle and natural way.

Below: Whatever your reason for seeking Reiki, you will receive a full body treatment, usually beginning at the head and shoulders.

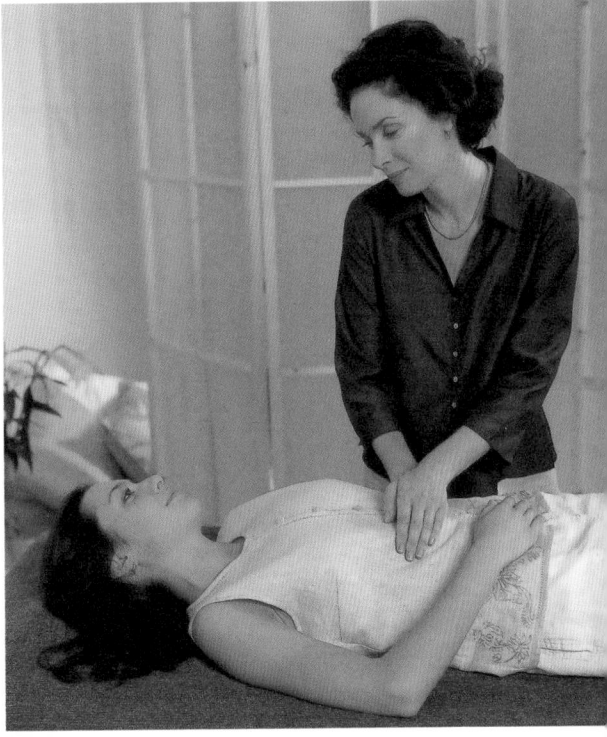

Above: Feel free to talk to the Reiki practitioner during a session, as things often come to light when you relax and allow your own healing to happen in this way.

## Surprising results

Maybe during your Reiki session you felt tingly, or saw beautiful colours or felt wonderfully relaxed, but find that your back is still painful or your knee still stiff. Remember, part of the holistic nature of Reiki is that it heals the whole. The beauty of Reiki is that it knows already where to go – the only thing that can possibly direct it is your higher self, in co-operation with the Reiki energy. Many people are surprised when they go home and fall asleep for hours. Sometimes a rest is just what the body needs to process and digest experience, or allow natural energy levels to recuperate. Conversely, some say that after Reiki they return home and do a big clear-out, or spend the afternoon working in the garden. And Reiki also nurtures creativity.

# Reiki Principles

Live in the world like water
on a lotus leaf.

YOGASWAMI

# Reiki attunements

You may decide you would like to be able to give yourself Reiki or help others with it, or both. Attunements are a prerequisite to practising Reiki, and an element of the teachings that set Reiki apart from other healing systems.

As a new practitioner, Reiki will not work if you have not been attuned by an initiated master, even if you already have other wonderful healing skills which will be complemented once you have been attuned. An attunement to the Usui System of Natural Healing is very often a landmark in a person's life, so profound and wide-ranging are the results. In choosing to be attuned, you are embarking on a journey towards healing your own being – physically, mentally, emotionally and spiritually. Attunements are a meaningful experience for both master/teacher and student; no two are the same. A Reiki attunement often helps people realize their potential in whatever way they choose to do so.

Below: A Reiki teacher sits with her student and draws one of the symbols in the air as she explains its dynamic nature. Many people feel a conscious connection to all life forming in their hearts following their attunement.

## An ancient bond

The relationship between master and student is a significant part of many ancient practices but a particular feature of Reiki in the Western world. Dr Usui received his Reiki attunement "direct" from his teacher, and it has been passed on one-to-one ever since. Important for both, the students can also teach the teachers a lot about the nature of Reiki. They are a blessing for each other – it is a wonderful thing to be able to share insights with someone else, and to know that another person is then empowered to share Reiki with themselves and others. A student will always remember his or her attunement to Reiki with great affection, for both the experience and the teacher's compassion and communication at this time.

## Preparing for attunements

There are beneficial things a student can do to prepare for attunements, psychologically and physically, at first, second or master/teacher level. For a few days before your attunement drink as much water as you can, to cleanse your system, and eat fresh, organic and unprocessed foods as much as possible. If you use recreational drugs, including cigarettes and alcohol, reduce your intake as much as you can. If you give yourself time to relax and contemplate your stepping into Reiki, you may want to experiment by putting your hands on yourself and feeling the sensations, so that you have something to compare with after the attunement. Take the opportunity to be in touch with any existing healing powers you may have which will be enhanced by a Reiki attunement.

Above: Reiki attunements can take place lying down, standing, or sitting on a chair with eyes closed.

Above: Receiving a Reiki attunement is like receiving an ancient blessing on your life.

## The physical attunement process

During all attunements, the Usui Reiki symbols are used to open the chakras and allow the person to become a Reiki channel. In the First Degree there are four attunements, but in the second and third degrees there is only one, so they are more brief. The student sits on a chair, eyes closed, with their hands in the prayer position, and the Reiki master/teacher moves round the chair throughout the attunement process. During your attunement relax and savour the moment. You may feel many wonderful sensations, from the exhilarating and emotional to the more subtle. Afterwards, you will be given time to absorb your experience and to return to the moment.

## After an attunement

In the 2–4 weeks following an attunement, your system will be adjusting to your new gift of Reiki and integrating the energies into your being. You may experience a healing process, and this is nothing to fear. Many people have all the symptoms of a cold, except the discomfort, as the body cleanses and balances its new energy system. Sometimes the effect is emotional and you may remember things you had forgotten, or feel tearful or light-headed. If you don't use it for years, it will still be there on demand –"Hands-on, Reiki-on, hands-off, Reiki-off", as Mrs Takata used to say. But the more you use Reiki, the more you will feel its healing benefits as your whole being begins a new lifestyle.

# The endocrine system and the chakras

The hand positions taught in the Usui System of Natural Healing aim to treat the recipient as a whole. If this is not possible for some reason, the Reiki energy will reach the parts most in need.

Attunements are created by placing the Reiki symbols within the chakras, to open the body as a channel. Chakras are also vital in the understanding of healing the whole person.

Chakra is a Sanskrit word meaning "wheel", and it is not unusual to feel a spinning motion in the area of a chakra, through your own hands or someone else's. Chakras are multi-dimensional, layered energy centres in our bodies, and, since the earliest Eastern representations, often depicted as lotus flowers. Most people cannot see chakras, although this talent can be developed. They are arranged in a central line along the body, going from bottom to top when numbered. They can be treated from the back or the front of the body and are often felt

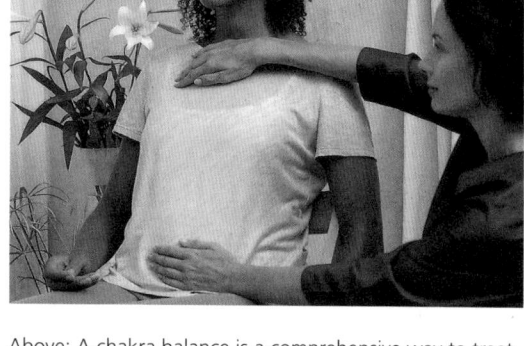

Above: A chakra balance is a comprehensive way to treat the body when there is not much time available. This kind of balancing is good for alleviating stress.

### The chakras and their positions

The following table lists the chakras and corresponding endocrine glands, and where they can be found on the body.

| chakras | glands | site |
| --- | --- | --- |
| coccygeal/root | gonads/ovaries | base of spine |
| sacral | leydig | 5–7.5 cm (2–3 in) below navel |
| solar plexus | adrenals | between ribcage and navel |
| heart | thymus | centre of chest beside the heart |
| throat | thyroid | middle of the throat |
| third eye | pituitary | centred just above eyebrows |
| head/crown | pineal | crown of the head |

as balls of energy. The functions of the chakras are many, and we are learning more about them all the time as we have further insights into the dynamics and significance of vibrational healing in all its forms.

Chakras perform their many duties in perfect synchronicity with our endocrine systems. This amazing system controls the functions of the body at a cellular level through seven major glands in the body, each of which is associated with a particular chakra. The energy frequencies at which our organs vibrate varies, as do the frequencies of our chakras. Holistic healing methods recognize that physical symptoms are just the visible result of imbalance in energy manifested at a more subtle level. The area of the weakest energy flow would be the area in which an illness manifests, an unbalanced chakra being the weakest link in the chain.

The seventh chakra, the crown, is located just above the top of the head. Its colour is violet and it maintains overall balance of the chakra system, stimulating fine levels of perception, intuition and inspiration.

The sixth chakra, often called the third eye, is at the centre of the brow. Its colour is indigo and it is concerned with understanding, perception and knowledge.

The fifth chakra, associated with blue, is located at the throat, and its concerns are communication, personal expression and the flow of information.

The fourth chakra is located at the centre of the chest and is associated with the heart. Its colour is green and it deals with relationships, personal development and sharing.

The third chakra, associated with yellow, is at the solar plexus, just below the ribcage. It identifies and assists in the sense of identity, self-confidence and personal power.

The first chakra, or base chakra is located at the base of the spine. Linked with red, it is concerned with physical survival, energy distribution and practicality.

The second chakra, linked with orange, is based in the lower abdomen, just below the navel. Its functions are creativity, feelings and sexual drive, as well as exploration.

## The art of synergy

The energies absorbed by our etheric bodies vibrate at a higher energetic level than those in our physical bodies. One of the main functions of the chakras is to decrease the rate of these energies as they filter downward, to an appropriate rate that our organs can deal with and use. In turn, the endocrine system sends out signals and relays energy to the chakras. Once in the form of chemical hormones, they can then be absorbed and processed to nourish our body.

## A web of life

Chakras operate on many levels; they are a feature of the entire Web of Life on a microcosmic scale in every one of us. While they are communicating with our endocrine system, they are also nourishing every part of our bodies with subtle, life-force energy, or "ki" as it is also known. Chakras are connected to each other and to our physical cellular structure by threads of subtle energy, called "nadis". At the same time, our chakras are fine receptors of psychic energy, picked up by our astral and mental bodies, which vibrate at an even higher rate than our etheric bodies. In this way, chakras are considered to have an important part to play in our spiritual evolution, as all energies picked up by our spiritual, mental, astral and etheric bodies are transmitted through the crown chakra situated on the top of the head and down to the lower chakras, which then distribute the energies to our organs. It has been found that organs with a similar vibration are grouped together with the chakra of a similar frequency, in a system of symbiotic flow.

# The use of symbols

The use of symbols is familiar to people of all cultures. Our first examples are often wizards and witches in fairytales, and later we learn that these tales have evolved from symbols in our own subconscious.

If our dreams puzzle us, we can often decipher them and realize that our subconscious minds are using symbols in the form of archetypes, which are the inspiration for the fairytale allegories we loved as infants. The psychologist Carl Jung rediscovered these archetypes after learning that the same symbols were significant to cultures the world over. They seem to be in the subconscious of the planet as a whole, and appear to have evolved with us. In our everyday lives, the exchange of rings is a symbol of eternal love, a circle with no end. When we hold our hands in a prayer position, we are symbolically sending up wishes and thanks to the heavens.

It is the intention behind a symbol which creates its energy, and endows it with so much significance. In a second degree Reiki class, students feel the thrill and power of the symbols

Below: The Usui Reiki power symbol has been found to work in healing, and empowers everything for the highest good. Its potency can be used in every aspect of life.

even before they are brought up to the level of the conscious mind by the attunement process. Walk into the power symbol or the emotional/mental healing symbol after drawing it in the air and you can feel the energy right down to the tips of your toes. The human race has reached an age when sacred knowledge is no longer the same as secret knowledge. Experiencing these symbols personally is an exciting and direct confirmation of their subtle power, today as much as ever.

A symbol can express a thousand words in a geometric or pictorial form. Many of us have seen a Reiki symbol or an astrological glyph and felt as though we have seen it before, or even doodled it ourselves, at some time in our lives. We may have thought we had done this absent mindedly, but can we be certain, once we have begun to research a little deeper into our psyches? The sign of the cross is recognized by everyone, but it also represents the flat, horizontal line and plane of the Earth, penetrated to its core by divine power descending from above.

Reiki master William Rand cites the ancient male and female Antahkarana symbols as the link between our physical brains and our spiritual selves. Rand's insights led him to believe that the Antahkarana is a carrier of vital, Kundalini life-force energy from the Earth. It is also said to carry ki (or "chi" or "prana") from the eighth chakra in our subtle bodies back down to the Earth again, making a full connection. This Kundalini energy is said to rise up our spines as we evolve in awareness. The Antahkarana symbol, whose origins are unknown, takes the form of a geometric shape, or "yantra", long used in meditation in Tibet and India. The male version is compact and focused, a symbol of channelled, directed energy. The female representation is expansive, showing a balanced and dispersed energy. Both are reminiscent of the ancient Hindu swastika and can be seen as cubes within a circle; if you look at them long enough, you can grasp the multidimensional qualities and sense of perpetual forward motion. The essential energy of the Kundalini is again represented in Tibetan Reiki, in which the symbol of Raku, the Fire Serpent, is used to balance chakras from the head downwards to the root or base chakra. This symbol also comes to us from China and other parts of Asia, and is used by healers.

The Usui distant healing symbol is used for absentee healing, bringing past, present and future into oneness. It has been translated as "The spirit in me honours the spirit in you." Today attunements to Reiki are even offered on the Internet; it is not necessary for a Reiki master/teacher to be present if we can use the distant healing symbol to such incredible effect.

Symbols cannot always be fully appreciated by looking at them on the page. Draw them in the air, visualizing them in their multidimensional forms. Often you will find you imagine them in the colours of healing (gold or purple) as you are creating them. When you do this, you are playing a part in the manifestation of universal healing.

## Reiki symbols

The first Usui symbol, cho ku rei, or the power symbol, with a clockwise spiral.

The second Usui symbol, sei hei ki, or the emotional/mental symbol.

Antahkarana, the ancient male symbol for increasing male energy.

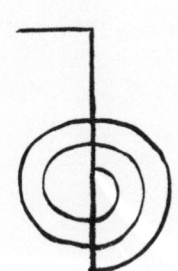

Cho ku rei with a counter-clockwise spiral.

Kundalini – the life force symbol from raku-tibetan reiki.

The third Usui symbol, hon sha ze sho nen – for distant healing.

Antahkarana, the ancient female symbol for increasing female energy.

# Intuition and bodyscanning

As you become more familiar with the practice of channelling Reiki for yourself and others, you will feel your intuition becoming clearer and the moments when you are aware of it will become more frequent.

Getting acquainted with your intuition is one of the most exciting things you experience after an attunement to Reiki. It grows just like any other part of your expanding self and its relationship to All That Is. Reiki gently frees old patterns of thinking, sometimes without you even noticing, and without the need for the brain to become involved. In so doing, the power of Reiki creates new space for continuing growth and awareness.

## Using your intuition

When you are channelling Reiki for a recipient, you may feel that a specific place on the body wants attention. Sometimes an area of the body can feel noticeably hotter or cooler than others. Your hands or fingers could start to tingle, or you might feel that you don't want to move your hands at all even if you have been holding them in a certain position for the usual five minutes

Below: Beaming from a fews steps away from the recipient means that the whole body can be treated at once, rather than via a specific point.

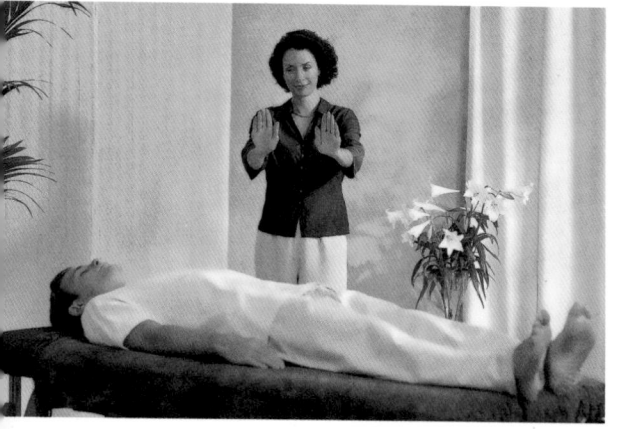

### Reiki angels
Angels and spirit guides do
not impose themselves on us.
Introduce yourself and ask for their
help and blessings.

or so. These are all signs that a particular part of that person needs the energy more than other parts. While we know that Reiki reaches everywhere, it is perfectly all right to wait until these feelings decrease before you move on and continue the full treatment.

Avoid scaring the recipient if you feel the presence of an imbalance or blockage. If they are suffering any pain or discomfort, enquire if they would like you to focus anywhere in particular. If they volunteer information about an illness or a specific problem, do recommend that they visit a doctor.

You may already be in touch with your inner voice or higher self or spirit guides, and perhaps you would like to ask for help from all light beings, or Reiki angels, to bless your session together. It is vital to ask the spirits for their help or blessing – if you remain silent or wait for them to come to you, you could be waiting for a long time. The spirits never impose on us, but wait patiently to be consulted. If it seems that nothing is happening, and you don't feel any warmth

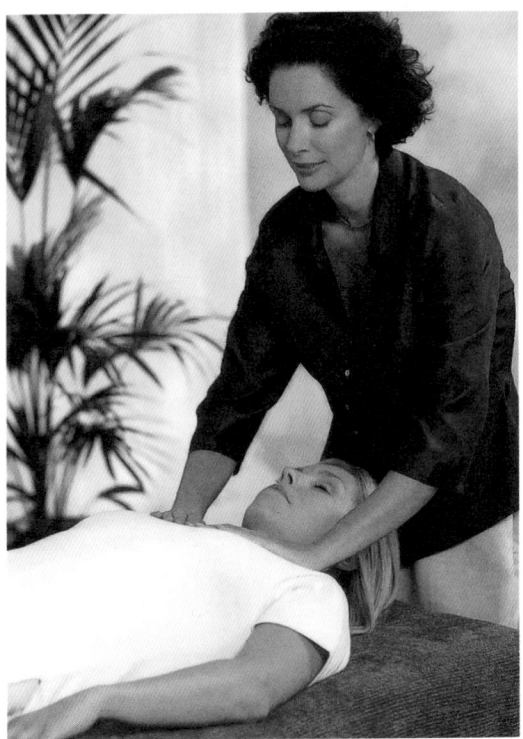

Above: Reiki practitioners sometimes leave their hands for longer over parts of the body where they perceive hotspots, as these can denote tension. Cold spots can signify blockage.

Below: A Reiki master will keep her or his mind open for messages and will listen to spirit guides and request their help during a treatment.

to tell you that Reiki is flowing, be assured that they are with you. A true request to the Universe always gains a response, so have faith.

Although the Reiki energy needs no help, I have asked the Reiki angels for love and clarity during attunements, and my more perceptive students have said afterwards that they had sensed that there was someone with me during the whole process, even though I myself had no idea they were there.

## Bodyscanning

Once the recipient is on the couch some Reiki practitioners like to scan a body as a way of introduction before a session. Some like to do it afterwards, and some do it before and after, to record any changes. If you explain your actions to the recipient, they will be more aware of changes too. The recipient may not have heard of this practice before, so put them at ease.

To scan a body, begin at the head or the feet. Holding one hand a couple of inches above the clothes, pass slowly over the length of the entire body, making a mental note of your observations. This is good to practise in a group at healing circles, and also practising on yourself will help you to explore and to gain invaluable insight.

Below: An energy sweep is a balancing and refreshing way to end a Reiki session.

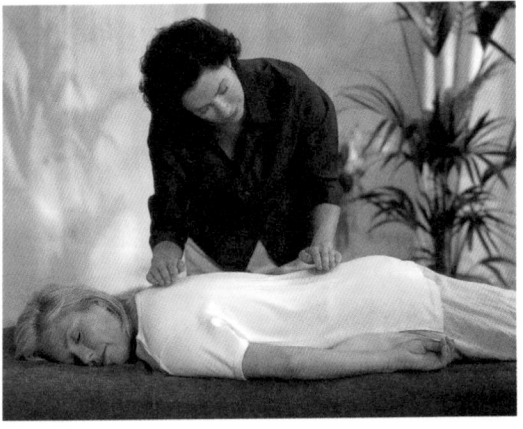

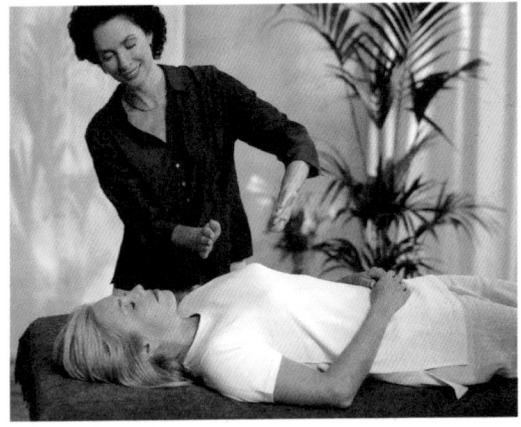

# Choosing a master

If you have enjoyed receiving Reiki, and would like to channel the energy for the benefit of yourself and others, you may one day decide to take it further, and learn how to perform attunements yourself.

Initially, you need to find the right Reiki master for you, someone who will gladly share their experience with an open heart in a way which appeals to you practically.

Today there are so many Reiki schools to choose from, and so much information within easy reach, that you can find us everywhere. However, as with many things, word of mouth is often the best way of ensuring you make the right connection. Although it is not always true that what a friend likes will appeal to you, many Reiki masters find that an attunement to Reiki is followed by enquiries from the recipient's friends and relations. Recommendations reach like-minded people, who are attracted to an energy akin to their own. "I had been wondering about learning Reiki for some time, and when I

heard about you, I just knew this was the time for me. I had to ring you. Will you attune me?" is a common response from people excited about practising Reiki themselves. It is often the case that someone mentions a new experience that you have been thinking of trying yourself. Reiki seems to find people, at the right time, in the right place, with the stunning synchronicity we are now learning is the nature of the Universe. Why else would people say with such certainty that they knew something was meant to be? It is good advice to say to someone seeking a master, "Ask the Universe, or God, or however you see the creative principle of life, for some guidance in finding your Reiki master. You will know when it is right for you."

## Something for everyone

If you browse online or thumb through the pages of health and healing publications, you will come across adverts offering Reiki attunements on a particular date, where a Reiki master attunes classes of up to 20 or more people over the course of a weekend. For first degree classes, two of the four attunements are given on each day, with the rest of the time spent discussing the theory of Reiki and exploring the multitude of ways in which you can use it. In the case of second and third degree classes, there is just one attunement; the extra time is spent either on the uses for Reiki symbols, or on expanding experience and learning how to perform attunements to the best of your ability and for the benefit of your own future students. Some Reiki masters offer the first and second attunements together in one day

Below: Many people meet at significant times to send distant Reiki and other forms of healing and prayer for the wellbeing of the world.

Right: A Reiki master will be happy to discuss the attunement process and other Reiki matters with you before you decide to proceed with a treatment.

*It is said that Reiki is a remembering, rather than an acquiring of anything new.*

or over the course of a weekend, so it is well worth discussing this possibility. Depending on your Reiki master and the size and duration of the class, some of the many different ways of applying Reiki will be discussed and explored after the attunements

Being part of a large class can be very stimulating. You will get to know other people who share your interests and with whom you can continue to network, or maybe even set up your own Reiki sharing group afterwards. Attunements are a powerful healing process in themselves, and often an emotional one, where hidden feelings may surface, so a large class can be exciting and supportive for all involved.

If you think you would prefer not to share your innermost feelings with people you do not know, a smaller class of two or three people may be more appropriate for you. Sometimes friends choose to share the experience of an attunement, and you could get a small group together if you all feel the same way. A Reiki master may be willing to visit your home, or

you may be welcome at his/hers. This creates a special occasion in an informal and comfortable setting where you can eat, drink and chat your way through the experience.

## Meet your reiki master
Many Reiki masters hold open days to encourage people to share questions, discuss issues surrounding Reiki and of course to experience some Reiki healing. Reiki manuals written by the teacher will often be for sale or on loan, and this is a valuable way of finding out more about your compatibility with your prospective Reiki master. Reiki masters will be happy to make an appointment to talk about their attunement methods, or you can talk over the telephone, or email. You can discuss things like financial charges or exchanges for a Reiki attunement, as well as where it will take place. If you feel the master is not for you, just wish him or her luck and say so. Even if you want an attunement on the eve of a full moon or under a waterfall, there will be someone, somewhere, for you.

# Using Reiki

The way is beyond language
For in it there is
No yesterday
No tomorrow
No today.

THIRD ZEN PATRIARCH

# The first degree

After the attunements to First Degree Reiki, you will be empowered to channel it for anything with which you have direct contact. Anything you place your hands on will receive Reiki simply by the intention to heal, and as you use it more and more this may happen automatically as it becomes integral to your being.

There are four attunements carried out in the First Degree, and it is often after the first of these that people feel a hitherto unknown sensation in the hands and a tingling in the feet. Sometimes the Reiki attunement prompts people to shed tears, or giggle or yawn, sometimes they feel slightly "spaced out", and sometimes it makes no discernible difference. The latter is often the case if the student has already been introduced to energy or vibrational healing at an earlier date. However you respond – and remember there is no right and wrong in Reiki – it is always a joyous experience and frequently a deeply moving one. This feeling of being "at one" is sometimes accompanied by seeing colours, or images of people or beautiful landscapes.

Above: They look the same, but they feel different: sometimes people feel heat or tingling in their hands after an attunement.

Below: You can bless all things with your new Reiki hands, including your food and drink. Anything energetic will benefit from Reiki.

## After attunement

Your concepts of hands-on healing will be expanded as you learn you can give healing not only to yourself, and other people, but also to pets, plants, food, drink and inanimate objects such as batteries, letters and computers.

Students taking the First Degree will have the opportunity to try out the traditional Reiki hand positions on themselves and each other during the class. They will also be given examples of short- and long-term treatments, and perhaps examples of appropriate positions for particular conditions. It is incredible to be given the gift of healing, and it can be overwhelming at first. If

Above: During the First Degree, your Reiki teacher will show you how to position your hands when channelling for another person or for yourself.

21-day cleansing process takes place in the body as energy filters and adjusts in the Reiki initiate. This process is reminiscent of how Dr Usui spent 21 days on Mount Koriyama, seeking the Reiki formula that would allow him to activate the energy. The Reiki is absorbed into each of the seven main chakras in the physical and etheric bodies (three days for each chakra).

Many Reiki masters advise prospective students to wait at least three months between accepting the First and Second Degrees, and often longer before deciding to become a Reiki master themselves. This is intended to allow the student time to process the experience of attunement, physically, emotionally and mentally. Some people also feel they would like to acquaint themselves with the physical experience of activating Reiki before becoming involved with the symbols and distant healing. Other people continued happily from the First to the Second Degrees, feeling it gives them more to work with. You can listen to the experiences of Reiki practitioners, but in the end you should follow your own heart.

you go home after an attunement only to sink into a spell of gloom or fly off the handle, don't worry – it's all part of the process. Place your hands on your stomach or head, or anywhere that feels comfortable. At this very special time, Reiki will help you to give and accept healing.

## The next step

Although Dr Usui is reputed to have passed on all his Reiki knowledge in one go, it is unusual to find a Reiki master who feels comfortable about passing on Reiki in this way. Although there is nothing intellectual to "learn" about Reiki, after an attunement to any of the three degrees a

Below: After the First Degree you can enjoy your Reiki wherever you are, and can even give it to yourself as you relax with a hot drink.

# The second degree

The Second Degree enables the practitioner to increase the power of hands-on Reiki, as well as sending healing across time and distance using the Reiki symbols given to Dr Usui on Mount Koriyama.

The first symbol, cho ku rei, is the power symbol, the second, sei hei ki, means god and man are one. The third, hon sha ze sho nen, is for distant healing. Attunement to this next level brings the symbols placed in the subconscious mind in the First Degree up to the conscious level, so that they can be used with awareness in as many aspects of your life as you wish.

## The attunement

There is just one attunement in Second Degree Reiki, the student having already taken the major step of accepting the Reiki energy in his or her physical body during the First Degree. This opens the chakras even more to receive and channel the Reiki healing energy. This Second Degree

Below: During the Second Degree you will learn how to draw the symbols, and explore exciting ways of using them to enchance daily life.

works on the level of the mind and emotions, which brings new opportunities to heal and to transcend mental and emotional problems. This, in turn, creates space in one's mind for expansion and growing spiritual awareness.

## Keys to creating energy

Following an attunement to Second Degree Reiki, students are shown pictures of three of the four symbols used in healing. (The fourth is taught at master/teacher level.) Traditionally, Usui teachers instructed their pupils to destroy any representations of the symbols before they went home, but now sacred no longer means secret, and the symbols are available for all to see on the Internet and in books, some of them in this book. The teacher's main objective when explaining the nature of the Reiki symbols is to convey the multitude of ways in which they can be applied. As the fundamental key to the activation of Reiki, they are all-embracing and can be used for every circumstance in our lives.

## The first symbol

The first symbol to be learned is the power symbol, cho ku rei. When invoked by someone who is attuned to Reiki, this creates the energy "God Is Here". As this suggests, this amazing phenomenon can be used to lovingly empower and bless yourself, other living beings, food and drink you take into your body, situations and occasions, inanimate objects and just about anything else you can think of, to startling effect. This symbol is often visualized on the backs of the hands while giving a treatment to yourself or others. It can also be drawn in the soil of an

### Sending Reiki

This can be done in as many ways as you can imagine. Here are a few tried and tested aids to channelling distant Reiki:

- Hold a picture of the person to whom you wish to send Reiki, or place it close by, and focus on the image while sending Reiki.
- Write the person's name on a piece of paper, as well as the date and time when you wish to send Reiki, and the place where they will be when the healing is intended to take place. You can speak these instructions too, inwardly or out loud. Draw the distant healing symbol, and the other symbols if you wish, over these written intentions.
- Give yourself a self-treat, and as you do so send it to another by saying inwardly or aloud, "As I heal myself, I am also sending Reiki to [the person's name]." You could continue, "My left side represents [the person's] back, and my right side the front of their body", or any part of them on which you wish to focus.

ailing plant, and in food with your fork. It is effective for clearing a house where trauma has occurred, or to welcome a new home. Paint it over your walls to give a joyful aspect to interior design, or in the bath for an invigorating start to the day, or in the classroom for a lively lesson – this symbol brings positive energy and life to every possible situation.

## The second symbol

This symbol, sei he(i) ki, promotes mental and emotional healing wherever it is called to help. One of the first successes I enjoyed with this symbol was visualizing its creation between the eyes of a boisterous dog during the lunchtime of my attunement to Second Degree Reiki, immediately after my Reiki master had cited this use as a good example. The dog was bounding towards us and just as I finished saying the

name of the symbol for the third and last time, it stopped in its tracks and padded on peacefully. This healing symbol can also be drawn in the air near a crying baby, as its energy is soothing and clearing. Draw it over or under your bed at night, or on a piece of paper to place under your pillow, and in places where there is conflict of any kind.

## The third symbol

This symbol, hon sha ze sho nen, is the only one needed to send Reiki healing over distance or time, and it transcends both, acting in the past, future and present simultaneously. The name of this beautiful symbol can be interpreted as "May the Buddha in me reach out to the Buddha in you to promote harmony and peace." In this way, we reach the essence of the object of our healing intent. Many people insist that people must ask for healing, and that you should not send it of your own accord. Use your own judgement in this matter. Perhaps someone is too ill to reach you, and you know the healing would be accepted with gratitude. Proceed with the best intentions and send your thanks to the Universe.

Below: Sending distance healing while giving yourself Reiki is a very effective way of practising.

# The third degree

Many people practise Reiki happily for years without ever feeling the desire to become a teacher themselves. Others decide to take the Third Degree for healing purposes only, to enhance their activation of Reiki with the master symbol.

As with the decision to accept any of the three Reiki Degrees, there are many schools and attitudes to choose from when you are considering becoming a teacher and passing on attunements yourself.

## The right moment

Judgement is sometimes passed by Reiki masters about whether a student is sufficiently aware to embark on the Third Degree, but, whatever anyone may tell you, this decision should ultimately be made by the student – even if that decision is to be guided by the master as

*All shall be well,*
*all shall be well,*
*and all manner of things shall be well.*
ST JULIAN OF NORWICH

Below: There is nothing academic about Reiki, but there is much to learn from the experiences of other philosophies and practitioners.

to when the right time is reached. If you have spent some time sharing Reiki with others, whether for friends, professionally, or both, you may well feel it is the right time for you. That is the time to contact your Reiki master, or to look for another master to attune you to the Third Degree. Although First and Second Degrees are sometimes given during the same course, it is advisable to wait a while until becoming a Reiki master yourself, simply so that you know what you are passing on to others – it is difficult to teach otherwise.

## Commitment to learn

Making the decision to become a Reiki master does not mean you should let yourself be pressurized by suddenly being thought of as a "guru", and open for advice 24 hours a day – asked for or otherwise. What we are really doing when we ask for Third Degree attunement is making a commitment to the spiritual evolution of ourselves and others on the planet, for we are all learning together. Taking the Third Degree is

Above: As with all attunements, you will benefit from giving your system cleansing space. Make a special moment by adding care or ritual to everyday activities.

who will mark them for you. There are also other Reiki masters who are in love with Reiki themselves and recognize the wish to be able to pass it on, especially at a time in the world when the more healers there are the better. Their courses may last a weekend only and you can discuss a suitable fee or exchange.

Everyone who decides to take the step towards Reiki mastership does so having found joy in living within the Reiki principles. They are honouring an inward promise to continue evolving along that path because they have found it constantly returns love and happiness to their lives. The desire to become a Reiki master signifies a trust in the Universe, and the underlying wish to shed the constrictions of the ego gently and with as little conflict and as much love and acceptance of oneself and others as possible.

a commitment to our intention to live within the Reiki ideals. The Reiki principles were written to empower us towards our own happiness, and they are included in every other spiritual teaching and religious school of thought in one form or another.

## Different approaches

More and more people are taking Third Degree since the explosion of Reiki in the Western world during the 1980s. There are so many kinds of Reiki to choose from that if you follow your intuition you will find one that is right for you.

Traditionally there is a period of training as a Reiki master, which usually lasts about a year. An Usui Reiki master may ask a candidate to accompany him or her on First and Second Degree courses, for which you will be asked to pay a fee (you might like to approach the Reiki Association for a guide as to what is a fair financial exchange for master-level attunement). During your apprenticeship, you may be asked to send essays on Reiki to your Reiki master,

Below: Keep practising your attunements and hand positions, even when you have reached master level, on willing friends or family members, or perhaps even a co-operative bear!

# Hand positions

The hand positions used in Reiki have been passed down through the lineage of masters and practitioners in the traditional Usui System of Natural Healing, and have many physical and metaphysical benefits, which will be explored on the following pages.

During a treatment, the hand positions are usually followed in sequence from head to toe, though occasionally people begin at the feet and finish at the head. Following these positions gives the attuned practitioner a method of treating the whole person in a comprehensive way. The positions are designed to care for the whole being, physically, mentally, and also spiritually, as you will remember that the etheric body has seven chakras of its own which correspond to the seven main energy centres of the physical body.

Reiki guidelines recommend three to five minutes spent in each hand position. Sometimes, you can feel intense heat or cold when you place your hands on a particular spot. Sometimes, your hands can tingle or feel heavy as the recipient draws in the energy, and sometimes you may feel nothing, in which case be assured that the Reiki is still working perfectly.

Below: The hand positions in Reiki are easily taught, and seem to be part of the intuitive, natural process of healing when they are explained by a master or teacher.

*The Spiritual Principles*

*Just for today do not worry*

*Just for today do not anger*

*Honour your parents, teachers and elders*

*Earn your living honestly*

*Show gratitude to everything*

If any particular feeling in your hands has not dissipated after five or six minutes, you can leave your hands in position until it does – although often if you leave then return to a "hotspot" after carrying out the remaining hand positions, you will find it no longer thirsts for the Reiki so strongly. This is because an imbalance may have been created elsewhere, and has now been healed at the source, or vice-versa.

## How to hold your hands

Your attunements to Reiki allow you to channel healing through the palm chakras, and in order for the energy flow to be focused, practitioners keep their fingers and thumbs together, and their hands flat or very slightly cupped. This may not be possible in certain circumstances, for example, during a couch treatment when you may feel that your thumbs are in the way around the throat area, or if you feel there is a risk of the recipient feeling uncomfortable. In cases like these, don't worry about the hand shape, the Reiki will still be flowing outward.

## Hand positions with recipient face up on a couch

Begin by tuning in to Reiki and breathing calmly in the present moment, with your hands on the recipient's shoulders as he or she lies face up on a treatment couch or massage table. This moment or two gives the recipient time to settle in and become accustomed to your touch and the treatment room. Once you have hand contact with the recipient, try to maintain contact until the treatment is over. The recipient will be more relaxed if they are aware of your body position throughout the session.

**1** Place the palms of your hands over the recipient's eyes, with your wrists just above the forehead, thumbs meeting at the bridge of the nose and fingers on either side of the nose on the cheeks. Gently lower your hands until you are touching the face. Centring around the sixth chakra, this position energizes the eyes, and aids clear vision, including the intuition. You will also be treating the emotional stress release points just above the eyebrows.

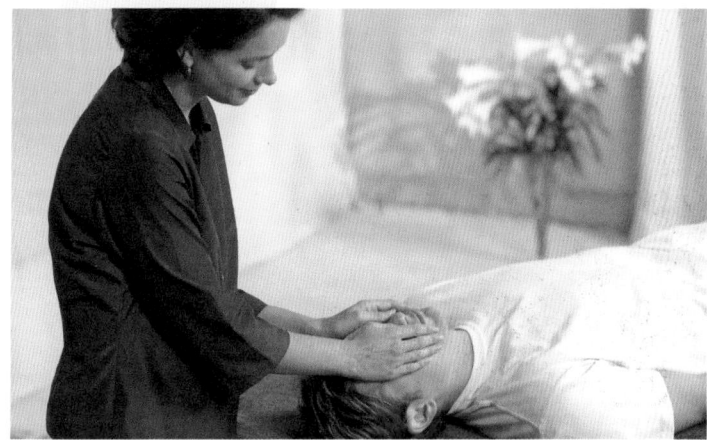

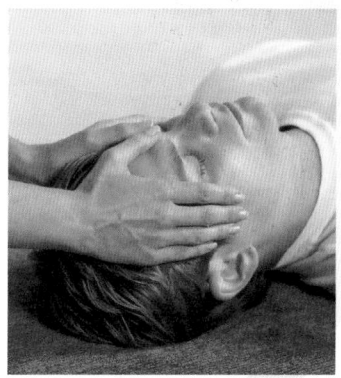

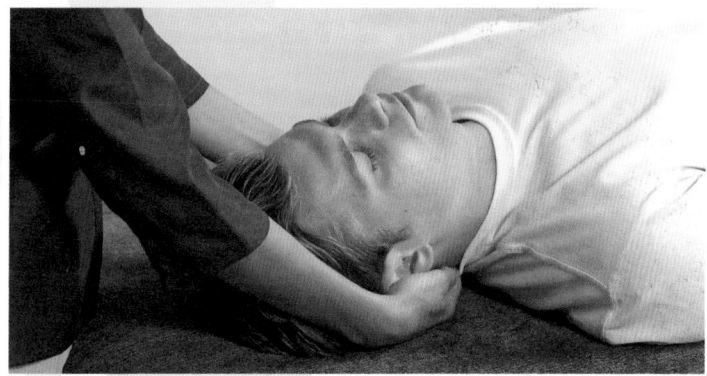

**2** Gently part your hands and slide up and sideways until your palms are on the temples, and your fingers just on the ears and the jaw area. This position helps to dispel tension in the face.

**3** Slowly slide your right hand from the recipient's ear on to their cheek, and with your left hand, gently roll the head on to your right hand, so that this hand is now flat. Slide your left hand underneath the head just above the neck so that you are cradling it. Your right hand can now roll the right side of their face toward the left, and slide underneath the right side of the head. Achieving this position change fluently can take practice, but once you are there you will notice how relaxed the recipient is when they allows the weight of their head to rest on your hands. It is amazingly soothing, balancing the energy in both sides of the brain and releasing mental tension. Visualize drawing the healing symbol on the backs of your palms while you are changing position.

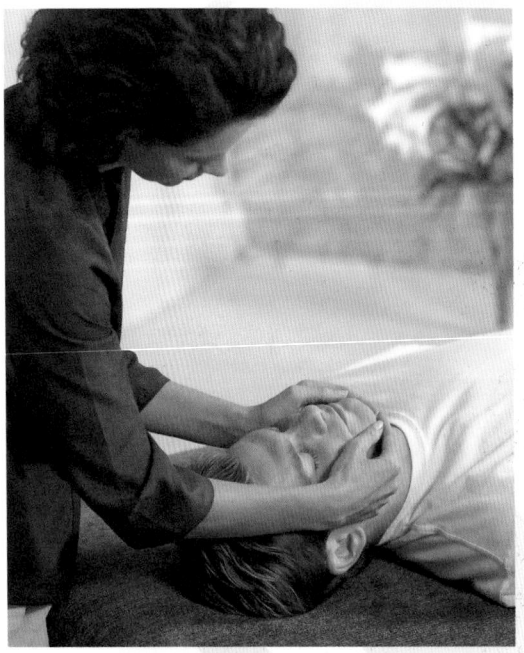

**4** With your left hand, gently roll the recipient's head to the right, so that your right hand supports it, and move your left hand down to the bottom of the chin and throat as you slowly slide your right hand out from underneath and guide the head so that it is again centred on the couch. Place your hands with the heels of your palms on the side of the neck and your palms and fingers lightly on the throat, overlapping. Do not place pressure on the recipient; you might prefer to rest your elbows on the treatment couch so that you are steady.

Alternatively, you can lightly place the thumbs on the bottom of the jaw and interlace your fingers over the throat if the recipient is not very relaxed. Either way, be aware that the throat is a very sensitive place, where the fifth chakra known as the "centre of the will" resides. The throat stores emotional memory and communication, so it is important to respect this. Be aware that in this position the recipient may get a lump in their throat, or tears may well up as healing occurs, releasing trauma and emotion.

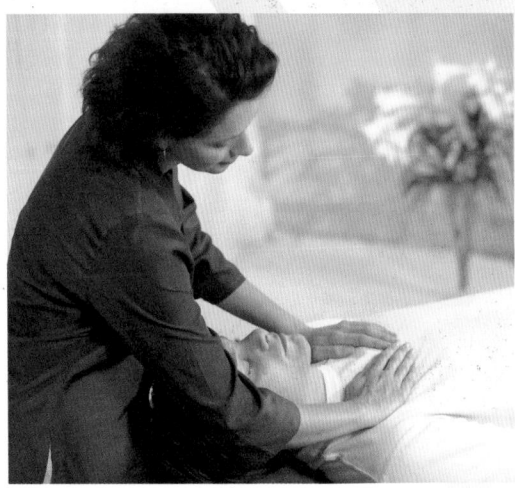

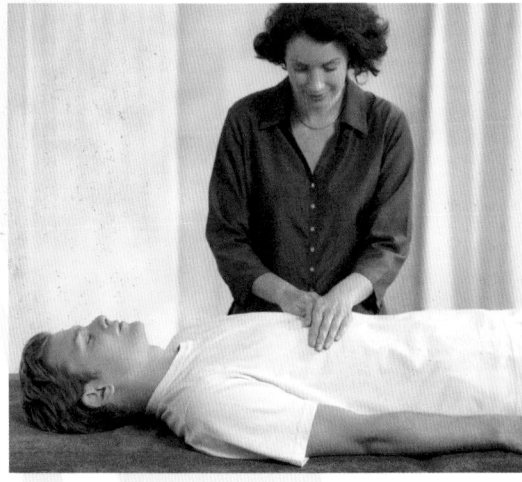

**5** Slide your hands below the throat, lightly outward on to the chest and towards the arms. Stop when the palms are on the armpits. This is not a traditional hand position, but I have included it because so many people love it and visibly relax, absorbing the Reiki into the lymph region. This is a great help in ridding the body of toxins. The position also treats the lungs and clears the chest.

**6** Now stand if you weren't already, and move to one side of the chest. Place your two hands in a straight line across the sternum. This is now the fourth chakra or heart area and Reiki here helps to encourage the recipient to love – both oneself and others. You can also hold both hands on either side of the body, always staying near the centre, for three to four minutes anywhere in this area.

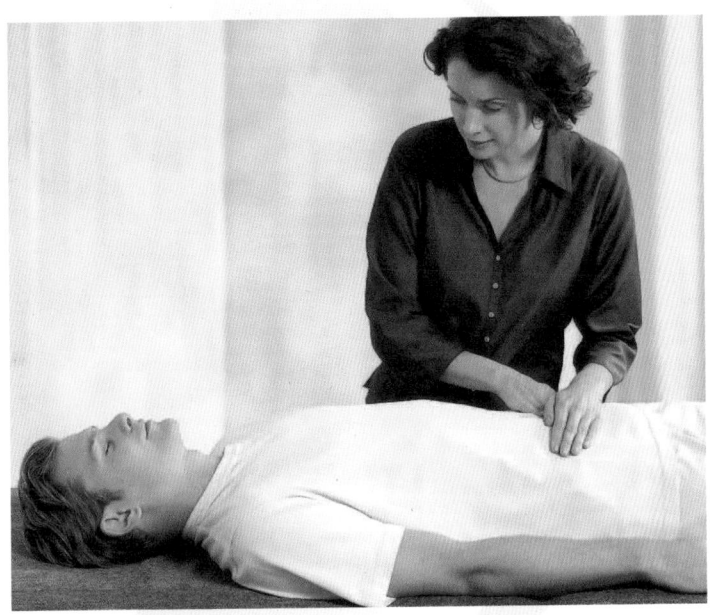

**7** Hold your hands, again one behind the other, over the chest area, continuing to give Reiki to the heart and lungs as you move downwards.

**8** Next, move the hands down, resting across the solar plexus area where emotions are stored. Continue downwards, resting the heels of your hands either side of the pelvis, with your fingers pointing upwards towards the navel. This benefits the pelvic area, and all organs near the second chakra. Finally, move one hand slowly up to the centre of the chest, ending the treatment for the front of the upper body.

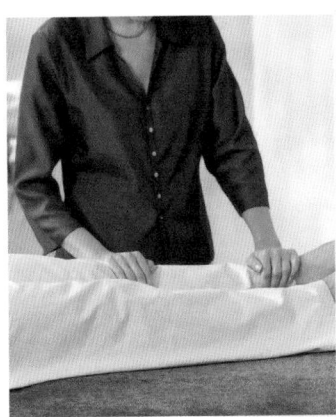

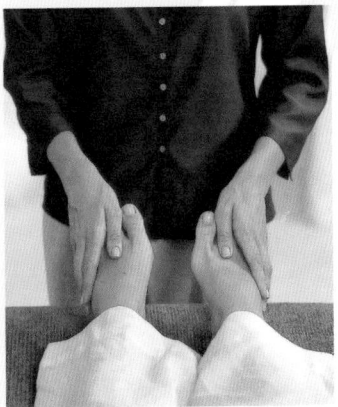

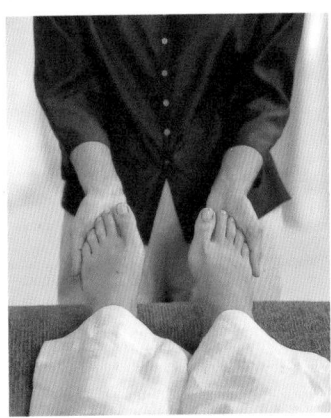

**9** You can then treat the legs, moving downwards in as many stages as your time allows. These positions relax muscles all the way down the lower body, and create a balancing effect.

**10** Treat the tops of the feet to bring awareness to the whole body, and to ground the recipient as he may feel slightly heady.

**11** The soles of the feet being so sensitive, this position can help to bring round a sleepy recipient at the end of a treatment.

## Hand positions with recipient face down on a couch

Reiki sessions can be successfully carried out just treating the front of the body, but you may also like to treat the back directly, especially if the recipient is having any problems in this area. Ask your recipient to gently turn over on the couch for this body treatment.

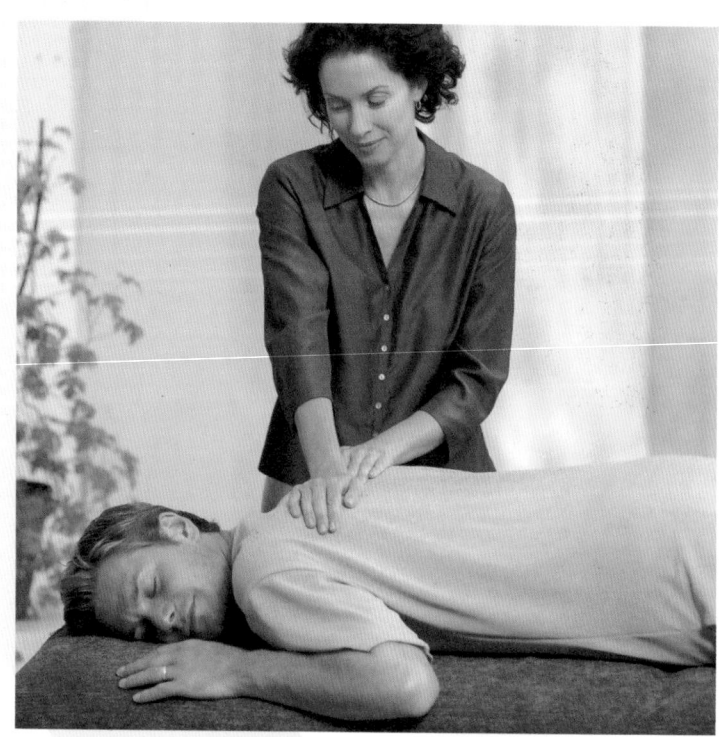

**1** When your recipient is face down, place your hands on either shoulder, moulding your hands to their shape. As well as introducing the beginning of the back treatment, this soothes and melts away any deep-seated tensions stored in the neck and shoulder areas.

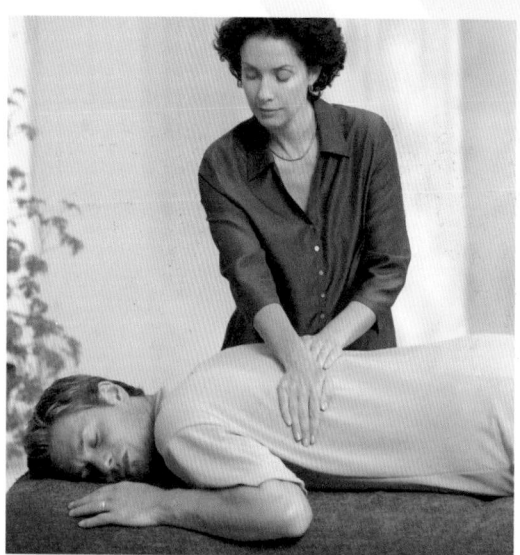

**2** This is not a traditional hand position, but again, it's much loved and, appropriately, works on the heart chakra. You can also follow this by making a T-cross, with one hand placed vertically underneath so that the heel of the hand is nearer the solar plexus.

**3** Gently move your hands outward, so that they are positioned on either side of the abdomen and solar plexus, moving down towards the kidneys, until your hands are either side of the ribcage. This position is a fabulous boost to kidneys and adrenal glands.

**4** Slide your hands down and together, so that they are in a small T-cross at the base of the spine. Complete the upper body positions by moving one hand to the top of the spine, with the other at the base. This will act like a spirit level, balancing the energy along the spine and gently rejuvenating the recipient.

**5** As when giving Reiki to the front of the body, you can now move down the legs and further relax muscles and joints. You can ask if there is anywhere the recipient would like you to focus.

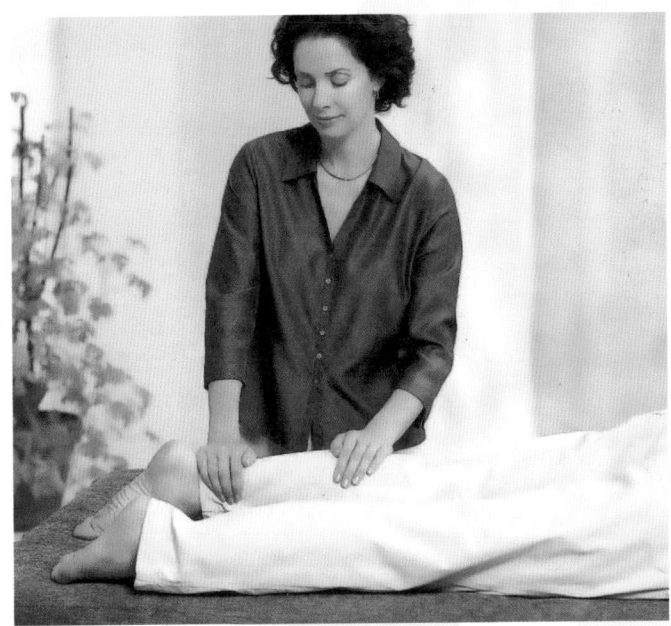

**6** When you have worked on one leg, use the same positions on the other.

### Winding down

End this part of the treatment by moving down to the feet, crouching on a level with them, if that feels comfortable. Rest your hands lightly on the recipient's soles, and then visualize the creation of the emotional/mental healing symbol. Then, keeping your hands where they are, imagine the outline of the power symbol on the backs of your hands. Now would be a good time to use the distant healing symbol before the other two, and send the recipient more Reiki for a further hour following this hands-on treatment.

## Hand positions for recipient in a chair

Sessions in a chair are often preferred by people who are new to Reiki; they are great for spontaneous Reiki treats, and also for anyone who finds it a struggle to get on and off a couch. Recipients should be seated straight, but relaxed, and the Reiki practitioner should find an ideal height, or back strain can occur. Check that you can move around the chair freely for all the hand positions you intend to use. Again, these positions are a guide, so go with your intuition.

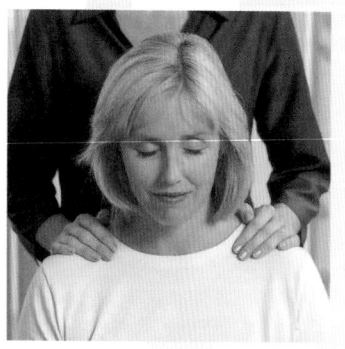

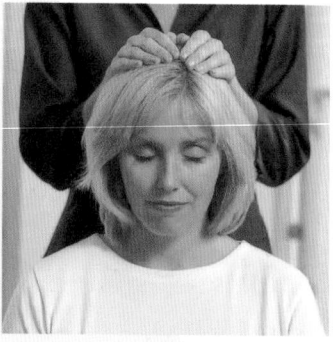

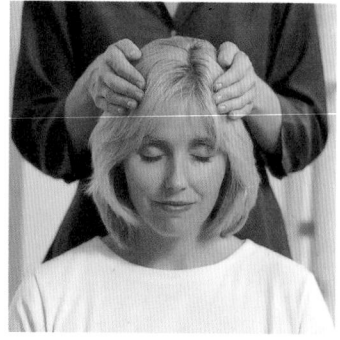

**1** First of all, lay your hands on the shoulders as you stand behind and tune in, taking a few deep and gentle breaths and resting your hands lightly on their body. You might like to draw the distant healing symbol in the air over the recipient's head, to send healing.

**2** Put your hands very lightly on or over the top of the recipient's head, as this position can be very stimulating. Only hold this position for two or three minutes, as this is the area of the crown chakra and is very delicate.

**3** Move your hands to either side of the head. This position is very supportive, and you can strengthen the treatment by drawing in your mind the emotional/mental healing symbol on the backs of your hands, followed by the power symbol on top of this.

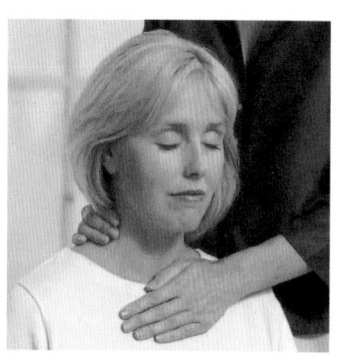

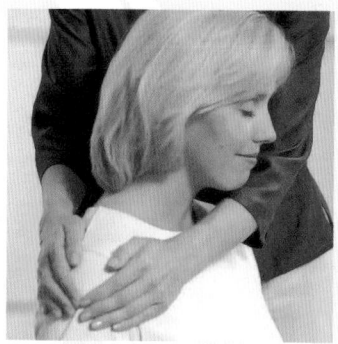

### Finish with the feet

At the end of the session you can use this hand position on the recipient's feet, especially if they are feeling slightly light-headed. Crouch in front of her, or sit on a chair facing her and take one or both of her feet in your hands, channelling Reiki on to either the tops or the soles of the feet. This will help to ground the person and completes a full-body treatment.

**4** Now move one hand and gently lay it on the throat area with the other hand at the base of the neck. You can continue to move down the torso like this, hands on the front and back, covering the chest and solar plexus.

**5** Now reach across the recipient to finish the treatment with the shoulders. Complete the treatment with one hand at the top of the spine and one at the base for the balancing "spirit level" position. You might need to crouch for this one.

## Self-treatment hand positions

Giving yourself a treatment in a chair is a great way to spend a free quarter of an hour. You could do a couple of the positions while sitting at your desk at work or in a quiet moment at home. If you have longer, use the time – it's never wasted if you're using Reiki. You might find that you only mean to give yourself ten minutes but then just don't want to stop. Let the Reiki take you where it wants to go and don't rush away. This treatment focuses on the head, face and neck.

**1** Place both your hands over your eyes and feel refreshed. This hand position helps to restore clear vision in strained eyes, and is effective for headaches and sinus trouble too.

**2** Place your hands on your temples to help to clear an overactive or tired mind. You can also treat your ears and jaw muscles like this. If your arms get tired, rest your elbows on your knees.

**3** Move your hands round to the back of the head and the neck area, dispelling tension and refreshing the brain. You might need to be in a more supportive armchair for this position, as your arms can tire.

**4** Now put your hands either side of the neck, benefiting the area of the thyroid glands, associated with communication and self-expression. This position treats the throat chakra.

**5** Place your hands above the breasts on either side of your chest. This position is very good for lymph drainage and clearing toxins from the body, so it sometimes gets very warm.

**6** Place your hands on your chest, fingers meeting in the centre at the heart chakra. This helps to transform emotion in the solar plexus to the heart area of unconditional love.

**7** Moving downwards, put your hands on your ribcage, giving Reiki to the solar plexus centre and all governed organs nearby.

**8** Place your hands about an inch below your navel, the location of the sacral or second chakra. This position is good for stabilizing tension, and also treats the spleen.

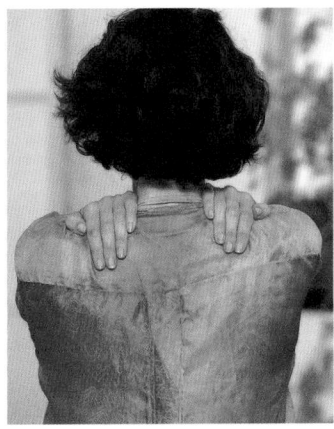

**9** Place a hand on each of your shoulders. This benefits the neck, shoulders and back. If this position feels awkward try crossing your arms in front before putting your hands in position.

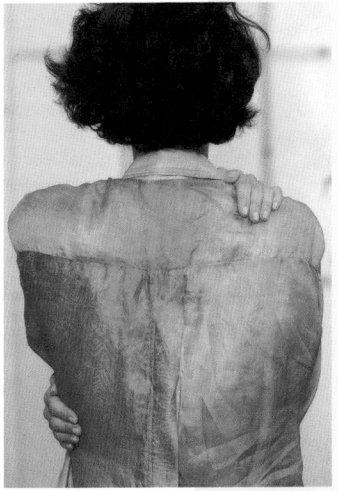

**10** Cross your arms and place one hand on your shoulder, and the other at the side of your ribcage, spreading the flow of Reiki down.

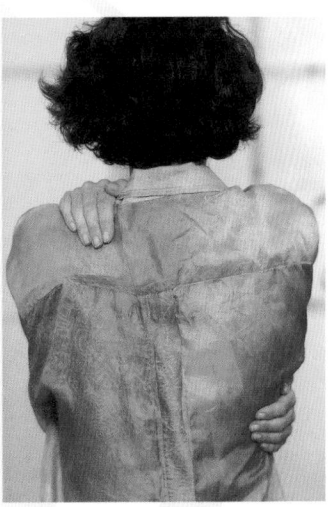

**11** Now repeat these hand positions on the other side of your body.

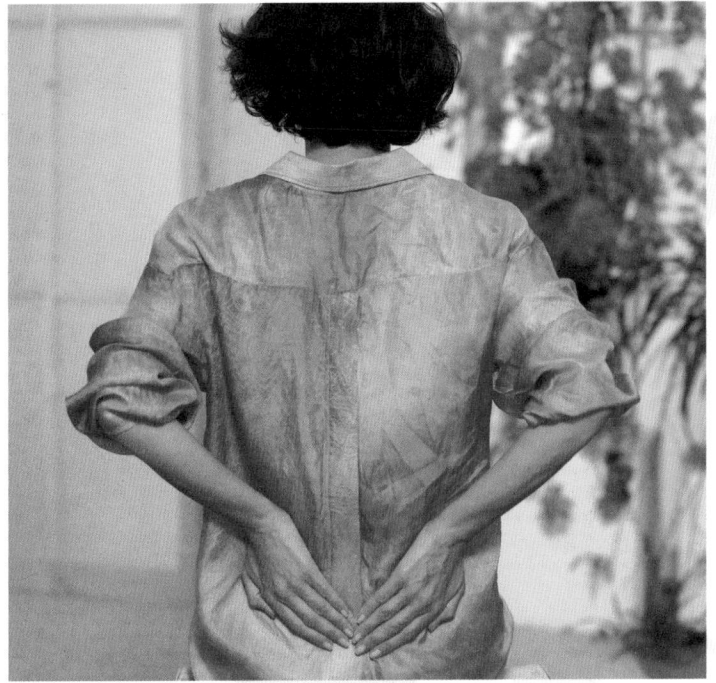

**12** Move your hands round to your lower back and place them over the kidneys, treating all organs cared for by the third, sacral chakra, including the adrenal glands.

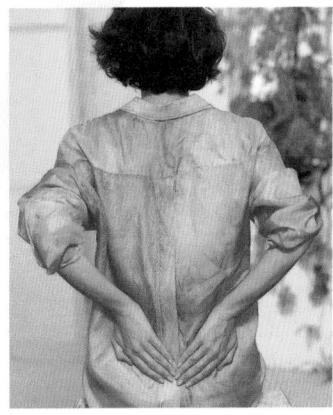

**13** Finally, move your hands lower to the base of the spine. Whether treating from the back or the front of the body, this position is beneficial for issues surrounding survival, will and fight-or-flight instincts. You can also finish a self-treatment by placing one hand on the forehead and one near the first chakra at the base of the spine.

# Treating yourself

There is one important rule about using Reiki on yourself – do it as much as you can. It will enhance your being in a myriad of ways, and we all know that the happier and the more whole we are feeling, the more good things we want to give to others.

Sometimes it may seem difficult to fit yourself in when friends and family are queuing for relief from physical and mental bumps and bruises. You may have even been motivated to channel Reiki so that you can use it to help someone close to you. However, this is a case of "Physician, heal thyself." The Reiki will leave you feeling as if you have had a refreshing shower each time you channel it through your being, but it is also important to nurture yourself with a long, deep soak. You will find that the symbolic gesture of giving Reiki to yourself is indeed a significant part of your own healing process. However, we are not always as comfortable about receiving things as we are about giving them. We may not feel that we need healing, and many of us hold the belief deep down that we are not worth it

*Sitting quietly,*
*doing nothing, spring comes,*
*grass grows.*
OSHO

Below: Spend some time each day enjoying life's gifts – sitting in the sunshine for a few moments will raise your spirits and link you to the Universe.

and don't deserve it. Reiki gently shows us that we are loved unconditionally by the Universe. It works just as well on a hangover as it does on a cold, making no judgements: our own concepts of what is self-inflicted and what is not are completely irrelevant to the Universe. One of the first joys of the gift of Reiki is the enlightening feeling of being "at one" that unfolds and envelops us, and is there anything more welcome in today's world than that?

Everyone is different, but when you give Reiki to others you will have more understanding of their responses if you have experienced it yourself. During our attunements, we learn that Reiki heals even when it is called on for the first time after five or ten years. You don't have to "practise" because you already have it, and there is nothing for your brain to "learn". The more you give Reiki to yourself, however, the more you can feel its effects, which is very exciting, and good for your confidence when using it with others. It is not selfish to begin with yourself, in fact it is important to do so.

Above: Making a self-treatment a part of your everyday life has a multitude of subtle benefits for your mind, body and spirit.

the other hand on yourself, you will benefit your whole being by treating your body and what you are about to take into it at the same time.

Some people choose to give themselves Reiki at the beginning of the day. This is the perfect time to thank the day for all the wonderful experiences it will bring, and will help you to live and grow in the Reiki principles. Just before going to sleep at night is also a great time for a self-treat – if you fall asleep, the Reiki will filter through. If you feel sleepy and want to avoid nodding off, sit in a chair instead. You can also visualize the emotional/mental symbol above your bed if you are feeling stressed, and wish to wake up refreshed and renewed. Any time you have your hands on yourself and are channelling Reiki, you can also be focusing the healing energy on dilemmas and questions you may have; make this your intention and wish for the best possible outcome. There are as many combinations as you can think of in which to enjoy the benefits of Reiki, so allow your imagination to create your own healing reality.

There is no substitute for setting aside a full hour for a Reiki self-treat if you can. Set your alarm clock if you have appointments, and switch off the telephone. As we shall explore later, Reiki works beautifully with other therapies, so you can incorporate it into a foot massage or beauty treatment. If you are having a busy day, give yourself Reiki as you go along – some of the hand positions are inconspicuous enough to enjoy as you stand queuing in the supermarket. Just put your palms anywhere on yourself and think, "Reiki Go!", as Mrs Takata would say. If you are watching television, you can put your hands on yourself and give some Reiki. Even if you have a drink in one hand and put

Below: Be aware of the physical and mental sensations you experience from different positions, while giving yourself a Reiki self-treat.

# Treating others

Two conditions should occur before healing can take place. There must be a shift in the consciousness of the recipient – they must want to heal and be able to assist in that process by having an open mind. There must also be an appropriate exchange (of money, of energy or of a gift).

Before your Reiki recipient arrives, there are a few things you can do to create a space conducive to this healing. First and foremost, you will be the one spending the most time in the chosen healing area, so make it a space in which you are happy and relaxed. Before the arrival of your visitor, take a few moments to ground yourself in the present moment, just as you do at the beginning of a self-healing session. Tuning your being into the Reiki energy before the arrival of another person will benefit both of you. You will be calmer and more assured at the outset of the session, and you will be able to focus naturally and with clarity.

## Preparing the space

"Smudging" or cleansing the air with a sage smudge stick is a fragrant way to prepare a

Below: Sounding a singing bowl is a lovely way to cleanse spaces before and after a treatment. You can also burn incense or candles.

Above: There must be an exchange of energy before a healing, so that both are participating in the experience.

healing room and welcome a spiritual and peaceful ambience. If you have taken your Second Degree, you can do this while also activating the Reiki energy in the room by drawing the emotional/mental healing and power symbols in each corner. Another lovely way of doing this is to draw the distant healing, emotional/mental and power symbols in the centre of the room, then visualize gathering up the symbols in your arms and scattering or sprinkling them outwards in all directions. If you draw the distant healing symbol in the air over the couch or chair, you can send your Reiki recipients healing before they arrive and throughout the session itself.

Wash your hands before and after each Reiki session – dirty fingernails are offensive, and your hands will also hold the scents of the day. Brush your teeth too. Place a box of tissues near the recipient in case they need one; you can also offer to place one over their eyes to absorb moisture and to assist with their focus during the session. There should always be fresh water to drink, and a light blanket in case your recipient feels cold.

Different people like different smells, so remember this if you use incense or essential oils. You could wait and ask your recipient which aromas they like from a selection of oils. Check that you are both agreed on the length of time for the Reiki session, and include a few minutes in which the recipient can return to the present with a hot drink. Sort out payment or exchange for the treatment before the session begins. Ask if they prefer daylight, or the curtains half-drawn or closed with a lamp lighting the room. Ask them to remove glasses, perhaps lenses, shoes and any jewellery. If you think you will want to take your shoes off, do so before you begin.

## The healing session

You could start at either end of the body, but Reiki hand positions usually begin at the head and work downwards, ending with the toes. Position a clock with a face large enough to see easily without having to twist or interrupt the treatment if you are unsure of the time spent on each position. A lightweight chair is useful if you are treating the torso, for example, and can do so effectively sitting beside the couch. Most people are quiet during a Reiki treatment, but sometimes people need to chat, or find themselves shedding a few tears or even giggling. Be responsive to comments, but try and say as little as possible. You can help the healing best just by listening, so resist any temptation to offer advice or anecdotes, as these may be distracting. Make the healing session a time when you pass on only essential and positive information. You are acting as a facilitator and Reiki is doing the healing, so the more supportive you are, the more healing the

experience will be. If you wish to know, ask the recipient if there is anywhere they would like you to focus on, but avoid negative words such as pain. By the time you are two-thirds of the way through a Reiki session, some people will have dozed off, so whisper when you have finished the treatment. Be gentle, and give them time to drift back into the present. Afterwards, ask if there are any questions they would like to ask or if there is anything that they would like to share.

When your visitor has left, turn the pillows over, open the curtains and the window for a minute or two, and take time to sit and be still once more. Thank the Universe for the gift of this Reiki session and dedicate it to love.

Below: Some people feel it is helpful to cleanse the aura by smudging as part of the ritual and ceremony of a significant healing process. Use whatever you and your recipient feel at ease with to focus thoughts and energies.

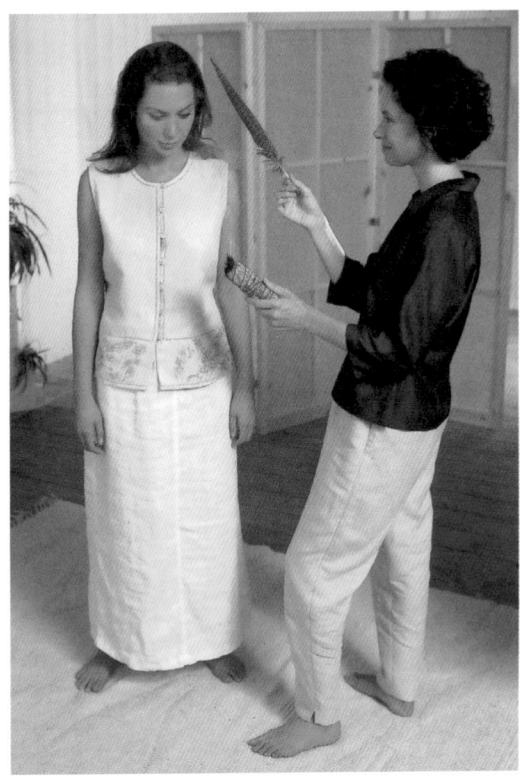

# The power of groups

There is growing awareness of the power of group healing as we extend beyond individual action in the Age of Aquarius. In this new era the emphasis must surely be on the importance of humanity working as a whole, and this is demonstrated all over the world by thousands of people who share the wish to help by using the power of love.

Some groups travel to war-torn areas to aid the emotional, physical and spiritual healing of the victims of conflict. Healing parties of various schools and denominations have been received by world leaders, with whom decisions of universal importance rest. As anyone who has used the Reiki distant healing symbol will know, distant healing, whether sent to an individual or to the planet itself, is also effective.

The power of prayer has been shown to work. People who have had near-death experiences report feeling and seeing the positive energy created by a prayer said for them. Hospital studies have shown that patients being prayed for enjoy quicker recovery rates, even when

Below: A healing circle provides an intimate way of bonding and charging up the Reiki energy before and after a meeting.

they are unaware of the prayers. The common intention shared by so many to raise the vibration of the world literally "lightens" the atmosphere. Motivated by unconditional love, we know we are operating from our hearts. This heartfelt wish has spurred people all over the planet to stop what they are doing at a pre-arranged time on a significant date, and to focus on sending healing to humanity and the Earth.

New physics continues to convince us that we are not individuals alone, but bundles of energy which overlap and meld with each other. Although there is no danger of contracting another person's ailment during a Reiki healing, people often see the auras of practitioner and recipient flowing into each other during a healing session.

Groups are also playing an increasing role in creating a peaceful planet in preventive ways. There are now academic research teams monitoring the efficacy of distant healing on decision-making processes in matters including nuclear issues. These and other projects show that we can enjoy enormous success when we work together, particularly as part of a healing group. Just sharing the intention and vision to heal means that the consciousness of the planet is transformed, because we are creating our own mass consciousness. As time goes on and we learn more, these kinds of exercises may well extend to group healings throughout communities. Teachers and children could be encouraged to take part in distant healing sessions at school, and we could see the day when they are accepted practice in

Above: A cycle of Reiki flowing between two or more people is thrilling and gently powerful. This sharing can be done for many reasons and at many different times, for support, healing, energizing, visualization and meditation.

hospitals. They would be especially beneficial in government and in the prison system – what a healing phenomenon that would be.

Healing is a conscious effort which is expanding, and it benefits us all to take part, for we are all part of a greater whole and we are creating our own future. If we think about when we have been most miserable, we can see that it is very often the state of feeling separate which causes us loneliness and sadness in life.

A healing circle is both a symbolic and practical way to experience the flow of healing.

You could do this with your Reiki sharing group before a session with someone who has a chronic or stubborn complaint. The infinite flow of a circle is bonding and will charge up the Reiki, activating it ready for a treatment. Afterwards it will give you all some extra healing time for yourselves, following which you could share your findings and feelings. Start up your own group with a circle of close friends and watch it grow.

There are Reiki healing circles in most areas, and you may be invited to join one already run by your Reiki master. Third Usui Reiki Grand Master Mr Hayashi is known to have encouraged and participated in group healings at his Tokyo clinic, and other forms of healing involving group ritual can be found in cultures throughout history.

# Group healing

Joining a Reiki healing group gives people the chance to enter the unique space that is created when a group of people with the intention to heal gather together. The loving energy emitted by a group of healers is so strong that it is tangible both to the people channelling Reiki and the recipient.

Sometimes people say they can see the healing energy of Reiki vibrating around the many pairs of hands while participating in a group healing session.

## Numbers and positioning

A shorter time is usually necessary for treatments when they are carried out by a group, perhaps half an hour or so. The time allotted to each person will depend on how many there are, but you can always split into two groups using two couches. A group healing session is appropriate for anything from two to ten people, basically as many as can place their hands on a body. This will not usually allow you to keep to the taught hand positions, but is wonderful for the

Below: There is no ideal number for a Reiki group – many hands are making light work at this healing session.

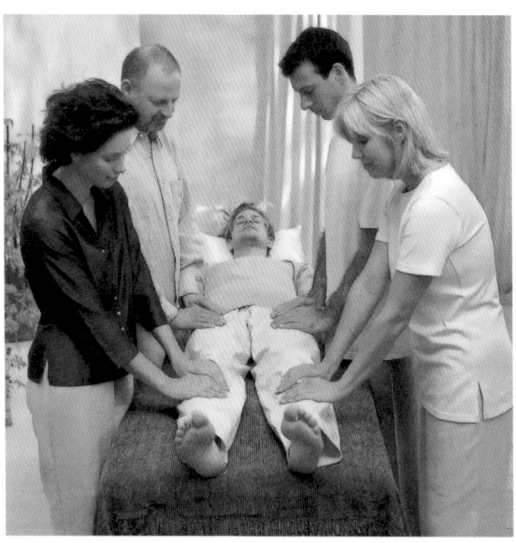

recipient. If there are only two of you, you can carry out a very satisfactory Reiki treatment in a number of ways, such as working from the head down one side of the body and around to the other side (following each other), or beginning at the head and the feet and working your way up, meeting at the heart and stomach areas. This will harmonize the chakras of the recipient in a balanced and even way.

## Opportunities to experiment

If there are too many people for one recipient, use the distant healing symbol together in another small group. You could send this healing from a different room or from the hands-on session, as both will activate the Reiki energy and further intensify the healing for the recipient and the rest of the group.

Another technique that works well in a group environment is "beaming". Stand a few feet away from the treatment couch and hold your hands out straight, with your palms facing the recipient (and the team in this case). Draw the distant healing symbol, the emotional/mental healing symbol and lastly the power symbol in your mind, and see them floating above the couch. Surround your visualization in a golden light and send Reiki to this healing; feel the energy radiating from your hands, and know it is filling the entire space with love and Reiki. This wonderful and enhancing healing technique treats the aura of the recipient, harmonizing imbalances before they even reach the physical body. "Beaming" is also an ideal way to work with someone seeking relief from a chronic or

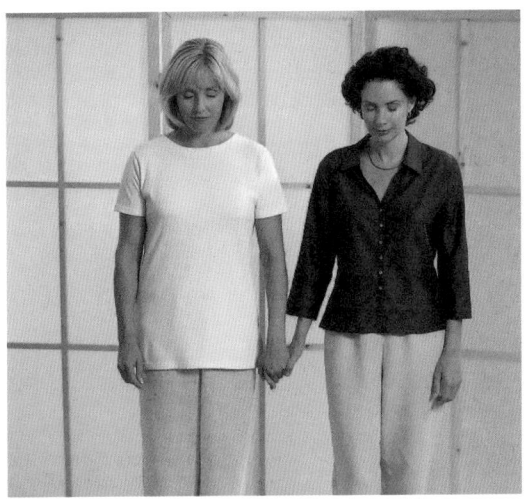

Above: Two practitioners focusing before the beginning of a Reiki healing session, and sending their best wishes for this meeting.

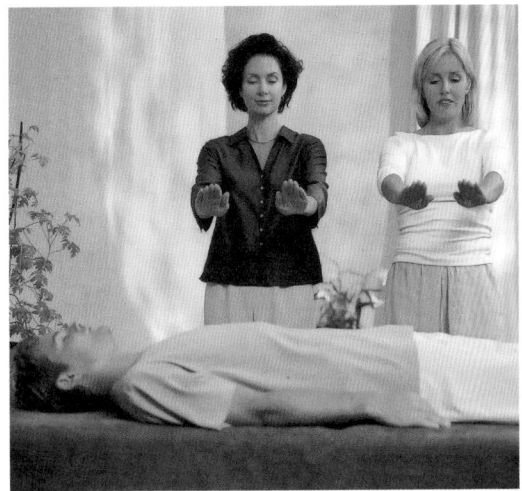

Above: Two practitioners beaming a Reiki treatment at the same time will increase the effect, and is a good way to use the combined power from a few steps away.

stubborn complaint, while they are enjoying a hands-on treatment. If there are enough people, the group could work in shifts for two or three hours. A healing group can meet as often as once a week to reap the rewards of powerful Reiki channelling.

A group healing meeting may begin with a Reiki circle ritual, a prayer to spirit helpers, a space-clearing ceremony, or a chant or song to invoke love and unity for the duration of the healing meeting. Some Reiki groups use tranquil healing music with a marker every 5 minutes, so that the group knows when to change position. Others find this a distraction and prefer to select someone who will keep time for the rest. Everyone is different, and communication is the key to a harmonious group experience.

Sometimes there will be people in your group who are also spiritual healers or shiatsu practitioners, or people who practise different kinds of Reiki. This makes it even more interesting when you sit down and explore your feelings afterwards. Reiki groups are a sure way to discover new ideas and techniques. There is a

great deal of scope for experimentation and for enhancing your experience of sharing Reiki, and complementing it with other healing systems.

Below: Hands can be positioned anywhere on the body or at the request of the recipient. Sometimes the group will work together intuitively, other times there will be guidance from one of the healers.

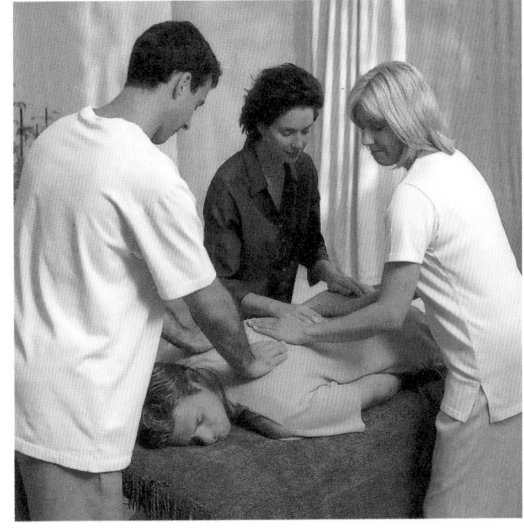

# Reiki Treatments

*There is nothing special
about what I do each day,
I only keep myself in harmony with it.*

HSUYUN

# Caring Reiki

Reiki is compatible with just about everything – complementary therapies, different religions, any kind of diet, even unhealthy ones, medicines from the doctor or chemist, inanimate objects – to sum up, life itself. Reiki practised with care can never do harm, and you can never have too much.

Reiki practitioners know that even for a healthy body Reiki is beneficial, its wisdom as ever guided by the Universe. I have never known a recipient to have anything other than beneficial effects. However, there are a few situations where contra-indications may be present, and where care must be taken to ensure Reiki is beneficial. For example, Reiki and alchohol definitely don't mix. The following observations are from experience but are not intended to replace medical advice and specialist expertise.

The most important things to ensure are that your intention is to use Reiki for the highest

Below: A careful practitioner will make sure she knows the details of a person's state of health, particularly, the use of any medications.

good, and that the recipient wants to receive Reiki. If you or someone you know is about to have an operation, ensure you send Reiki before or after the time of surgery. Reiki can cause changes in consciousness which may be incompatible with a general anaesthetic. The important thing to remember is not to send Reiki when someone is about to be anaesthetized, is in theatre or is not yet conscious after an operation. When recovering from an operation, though, Reiki will lift the spirits, accelerate healing and do whatever needs to be done, and most hospital personnel are happy to see family and friends helping a patient in this way.

People with diabetes should keep a close eye on their insulin level if they wish to receive Reiki, in case the Reiki causes the insulin in their bodies to fluctuate.

There are different kinds of pacemaker devices to aid the heart, and more care is needed with some than with others. Pacemakers that kick in when the heart rate falls below a certain level are normally compatible with hands-on Reiki and distant healing, and great benefits have been known in these cases. Reiki practitioners need to exercise more caution if the recipient wears the kind of pacemaker that operates all the time, as Reiki could affect the heartbeat mechanism.

Broken bones can heal so quickly under the influence of Reiki that it is essential they are set correctly before a healing session takes place. An ill-set bone may have to be broken and re-set if the Reiki healing takes place too soon.

If you are giving Reiki to someone with a gash or burn, make sure you place your hands above

Above: If a body is sensitive, or even painful to touch, or the recipient suffers from a condition such as diabetes, healing Reiki can be beamed or sent.

Right: Heat energy from Reiki can sometimes be felt through bandages, several layers of clothing, and even plaster casts.

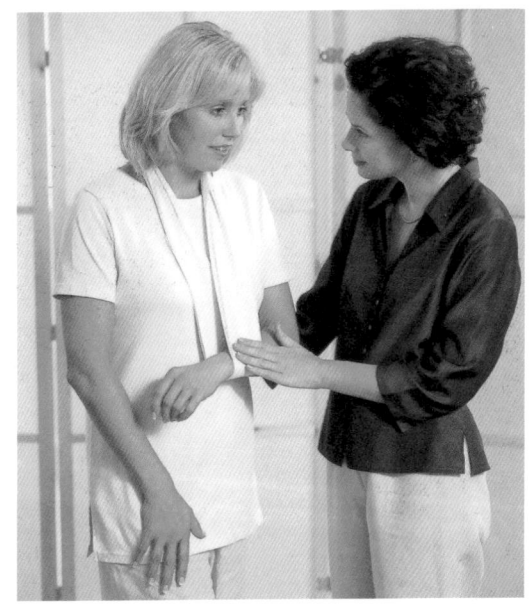

rather than touching directly to minimize the risk of infection. But recipients appreciate healing Reiki if they are in pain.

Interestingly, I have noticed that when I accidentally burnt myself and then channelled some healing Reiki, the sensation of being burned returned before the pain calmed and then ceased, almost like a physical mirror-image of the original burn.

# Patterns of healing

By wanting to heal, we take the first steps towards transformation and wholeness. With the faith that we can assist our own healing, we create a revolution in our minds, changing our pattern of consciousness from one of being a victim to one of growing empowerment. We are all transformers, and living with Reiki creates change.

If you are receiving Reiki through someone else, or if you are about to be attuned or have recently been attuned, you may find that you experience a healing process. This can be a disconcerting sensation, and there are ways in which you can support your being during healing, to ease this time and speed it up.

First Degree Reiki, empowering a person to channel hands-on healing, is often regarded as a time for physical healing, when a supportive nutritional diet is especially important. Second Degree Reiki, with its use of the symbols and distant healing, is said to be a time for mental and emotional healing. With the decision to take Third/Master Degree Reiki, you make a commitment to your own spiritual growth.

Below: Giving yourself Reiki regularly allows our true selves to co-operate with its energy.

Everyone is different, and you may find something easy while others may not. Whatever happens, and however strange or fearful a situation might seem, love and be honest with yourself. Thank any symptoms, quietly or out loud, for showing you that something is happening at a more subtle level, and say that you are willing to learn its origin and to release the pattern of thought which is the cause.

Sometimes after a Reiki healing session there is a resurgence of an old physical pain or emotional hurt. This is why Reiki practitioners generally like you to receive four healing sessions on consecutive days, no matter what the complaint. This gives the practitioner and the recipient time to deal with anything that may re-surface once the healing process has begun, and allows time to dispel the pain or hurt.

For instance, a man who had suffered with migraines for 20 years turned up for our second session complaining of pain in his kidneys. He said he had always intended to drink more water, and now his kidneys were shouting an answer to him. Since he stopped dehydrating, he has not had a full migraine and his headaches are now also rare. Sometimes Reiki can provide the fresh perspective necessary.

A few weeks before my attunement to First Degree Reiki, I hurt my back lifting. A week later I was working in a store with the doors open on a cold day. That night, what had at first felt like a chill in my teeth had spread to my entire face, and I have never felt pain like it. I could not think of a cause. A few days later, after no relief from prescribed painkillers, I began to try

Above left and right: Gentle exercise helps to cleanse the system too, while increasing awareness of your whole being. If your time is limited, just try some gentle stretching movements each morning.

other complementary therapies. Reflexology helped ease my back and my body reacted strongly to the lymph system hand position, as it cleared out toxins. However, my entire jaw was still stinging; I was in agony when I saw a sign offering Reiki in a shop window. No better time to put receiving Reiki to the test before my own attunement, I thought. The practitioner advised me that it was quite usual to have what was known as a "healing crisis" before becoming a channel for Reiki, and the treatment took the edge off the pain. By the time my First Degree date came, the pain had disappeared. It was a milestone for me to recognize that my pain had more to do with mental patterns, and it dawned on me what it meant to take responsibility for myself. With that, my own healing began. Being able to transform pain into an empowering experience showed me what adventure in my life could be about.

Taking responsibility for your own healing is helped by choosing to take good things into your body. Reiki practitioners often ask recipients to drink more water before and after healing sessions. After an attunement people may not feel like eating processed (or even cooked) foods and they may go off caffeine, alcohol and cigarettes. At this time, we are assimilating and integrating the Reiki energy and our bodies begin to consciously choose what is beneficial.

Below: Eating organic and raw food as much as possible is refreshing and cleansing.

# Reiki 'first aid'

When you practise Reiki, there are opportunities to help in a practical way when encountering unexpected situations or moments when help is needed. This is not to replace medical assistance but to offer healing and emotional support.

There are things you can do to help in such a situation, apart from safety considerations and medical first aid which should always take priority. Once help is on the way, you could channel healing Reiki, perhaps while waiting for the ambulance to arrive or even if you are simply stuck in traffic waiting to continue your journey. Any Reiki is better than none, and could mean that people are in a better state when medical help arrives. If you are stuck on the sidelines and feeling helpless, you can send up healing light energy instead of the negative grey clouds created by feelings of fear and anxiety.

*Man is made by his belief.*
*As he believes, so he is.*
BHAGAVAD GITA

Below: Every living thing has a healing energy guided by the Universe. Use Reiki to channel the positive life force during times of trauma.

### Reiki help
If you have taken Second Degree Reiki, you will know that you are also sending a prayer when you send healing over distance or time.

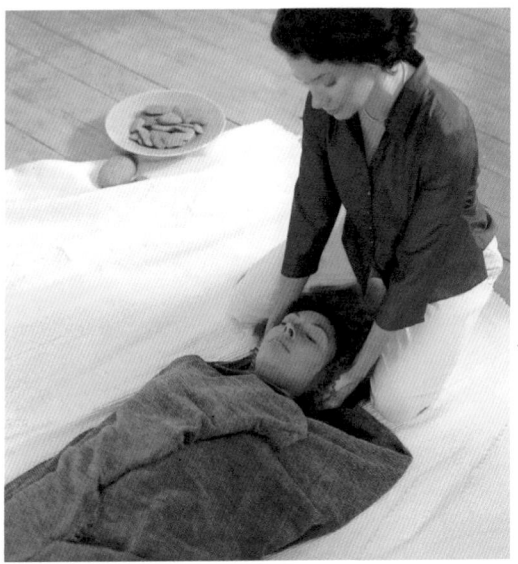
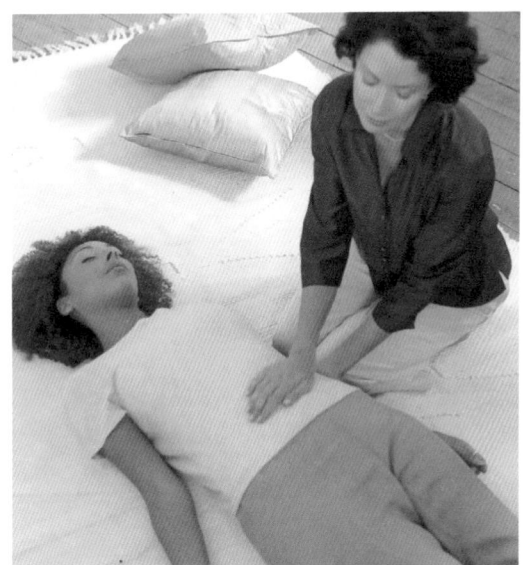

Above left and right: Keeping the recipient warm in a blanket and the comfort of Reiki will help after a shock or trauma, even some time afterwards. Simply placing your hands in the shoulder and neck area is potentially beneficial but take care not to move the head. Holding the stomach is also calming.

By offering your healing intention up to the Universe for the best possible outcome, you are offering the power of a prayer from the heart. If you drive past an accident, you can visualize the emotional/mental healing symbol in the air in the surrounding atmosphere. If you are in your car waiting to pass, make the distant healing symbol and also the emotional/mental and power symbols. Focus on the situation in a neutral way, letting the Reiki flow where it is most needed.

If you are nearby and can give a Reiki touch to someone feeling pain or fear, so much the better. Your physical contact through Reiki will comfort and heal, whether you are touching the afflicted area or not. If you carry Rescue Remedy, give the bottle some Reiki for a few minutes before giving it to the people involved in the accident. Then place your hands on the person's shoulders if you can, allowing Reiki to facilitate their own healing and to reduce trauma and shock. This position also feels very supportive. If given the

medical clearance to do so, perhaps you are able to kneel at the person's head, cupping it carefully and gently in both your hands to comfort and stabilize the brain energy. You can also place one hand over the forehead, rather than on it, to cover the emotional stress release points just above the eyebrows.

Below: Sending a Reiki distant healing prayer.

# Reiki for common ailments

One of the simplest and most instantly effective ways of using Reiki is in the treatment of common, everyday ailments. Using Reiki energy to focus attention on the problem areas, we can help to relieve and offer comfort.

Anyone attuned to Reiki will tell you how surprised they have been at the rapid relief a short self-treatment can bring from a common cold, headache or indigestion. On the one or two occasions I have had a cold since being attuned to Reiki, friends have taken the opportunity of experimenting and have sent me some Reiki from a distance. What has happened is nothing short of amazing – one minute I have been feeling lightheaded and sneezing, the next I have been trying to remember when exactly my symptoms disappeared without trace. Reiki

Below: Channelling healing Reiki energy through the spine is a powerful tool.

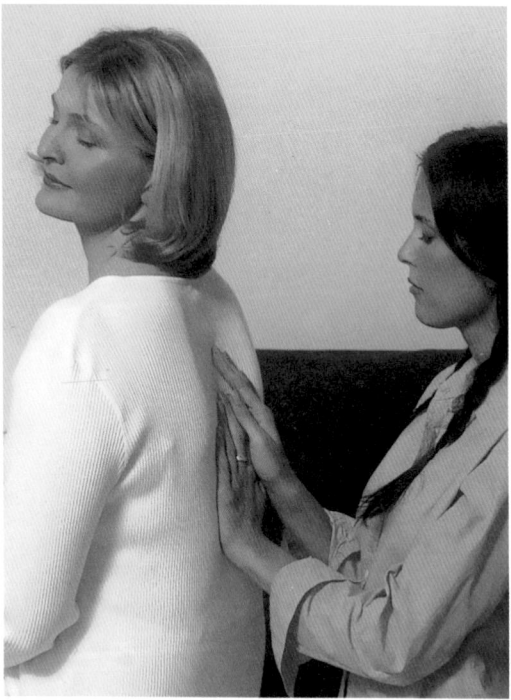

energy is so quick, yet so subtle, that some ailments fade away almost imperceptibly, just as emotional hurts can whenever you send Reiki to a situation.

Reiki treatments for common complaints can help us consider with calm insight the causes of our ailments. Reiki's greatest gift to us is empowerment to take responsibility for ourselves and our own healing, and that often means being able to recognize issues in our lives which, if not resolved, can make us ill. Many of us find that physical illness is the visible result of "dis-ease" created by negative belief systems that are causing conflict in our lives. Sometimes the mental and emotional origins of an illness can be hard to see, and even harder to accept, especially if we feel judged and vulnerable. But recognition of the causes of illness is a blessing, and certainly no reason to be judgemental towards ourselves or others, which can bring no positive results. The way in which many of us grow up competing with and comparing ourselves to others, nurturing fear rather than love, makes criticism a "normal" reaction, and a habit we must wish to leave behind as a beginning to healing ourselves. Criticism has never been found to help the healing process, but it can make us ill if our bodies hear enough of it.

The following hand positions can be held for as long as necessary or comfortable. You can also suggest to the recipient that distant healing sent to the source of the complaint will be very beneficial, and add this to a hands-on treatment if they agree. In your mind, create the distant symbols (emotional, and power too if you wish) over their head or on the backs of your hands.

## Menstrual pains

You can crouch down or your recipient may be willing to stretch out on a sofa, in which case you can slide one hand underneath her, which is very supportive. Place one hand on the lower stomach and the other on the lower back for relief from pain and stomach cramp. This will lighten and relieve the surrounding area, including the thighs.

Women who suffer from menstrual pains can use this Reiki time to celebrate the unity of females in the world and the expression of female energy.

Right: Hands on the back and front of the abdominal area are a good way to relieve menstrual pains.

## Backache

Ask your recipient to sit on a backless chair or to lie on their stomach, then place your hands together in the shape of T-cross between the shoulder blades and down the spine, to release tension and worry. Place your hands at the top and bottom of the spine to balance energy along the backbone.

Backache is often caused by worrying and feeling burdened. Lower back pain can indicate insecurity in material matters; such as worry about money. Trust in the Universe, which gives you everything, and know that your security will grow if you do.

Above: Back pains can be soothed away with the spirit level position.

Above: A T-cross made with the hands will treat back and shoulder areas, and stimulate the heart chakra and surrounding organs.

## Headaches

Stand behind the recipient and place your hands lightly on or over her eyes, your fingers meeting at the nose or overlapping. Placing both hands on the sides of the head at the back feels very supportive and dispels tension rising from the neck, balancing energy in the brain. Treating a headache by placing one hand on the forehead and one on the base of the neck at the back of the head, is also effective.

Headaches have many possible sources, including eye strain, sexual tension, an exaggerated need for perfection, and issues relating to how we face the world and feel about ourselves.

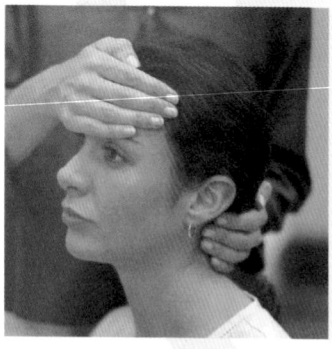  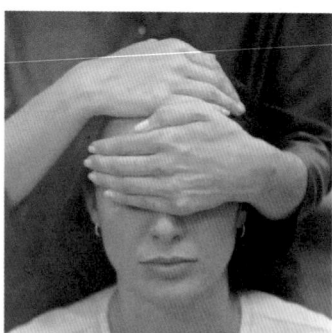

Above: Melt away tensions in the neck which can result in headaches with this supportive position.

Above: These two hand positions are very effective when relief is needed from migraine, eye strain or from stressful situations.

## Toothache, neuralgia and earache

Standing behind the recipient, gently put both hands across the cheeks, your fingers meeting at the nose or overlapping. Sometimes hands over the head, ears and face can also be very helpful, easing tension caused by frowning and unnatural jaw pressure. Teeth problems and neuralgia may originate from trifling worries or may be the result of anger stored in the jaw, often originating from guilt surrounding communication issues. Placing your hands carefully over the throat can be helpful.

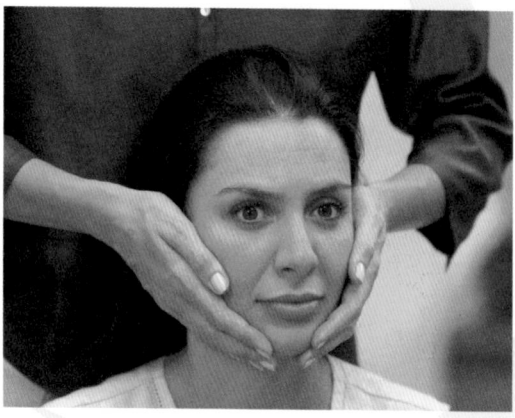 

Above: Cup your hands around the jaw area for toothache, and also for symptoms created by headcolds.

Above: Hands over the ears are warming, lightening a painful earache.

## Colds

Stand behind the recipient, and place one hand on the forehead and one hand on the centre of the chest. This will help to clear both and to bring relief from an aching neck and shoulders, stuffiness and coughing. It also covers the heart chakra, aiding self-nourishment.

Both hands over the face will help to clear sinuses and ease irritation. Someone who has received Reiki for a cold may find they also want to explore the emotional origins of their exhaustion, or if the cold could be due to a cleansing process by their body at this time.

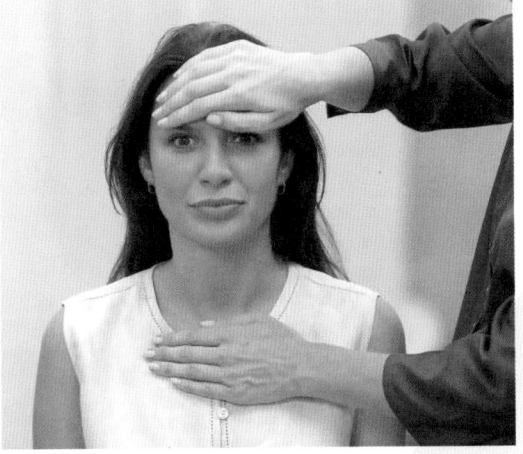

Left and above: Heads and chests are often very uncomfortable when we have colds. These two hand positions help to free sinus blockages.

## Indigestion

Crouch beside the recipient and place one hand on the sternum and one on the solar plexus at the centre or bottom of the ribcage, to aid stomach acid and general digestion. Place one hand lower down in the region of the second chakra for a upset stomach, constipation or diarrhoea.

Most indigestion is obviously felt after meals, especially with certain dry foods. It is worth thinking about any emotions we are finding it hard to digest and process. If you are constipated, ask the Universe to help you release everything you no longer need. If you have diarrhoea, ask what you are fearing in life, or finding it hard to carry?

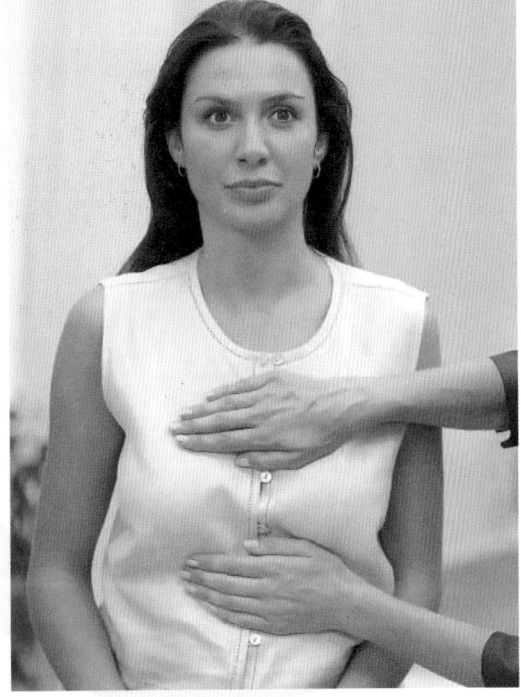

Right: These hand positions aid the digestion of food and can also help to free any blockages that are caused by the tension of emotional problems.

# Reiki in pregnancy

Throughout pregnancy and during the birth, Reiki blesses mothers and their babies with universal love and healing. What could be better than to put your hands on yourself and know you are healing and giving love to yourself and your unborn baby?

For both expectant parents, Reiki provides a unique opportunity to bond with the baby in its mother's womb, building a strong and spiritual relationship before this tiny new being enters the world and sees you for the first time.

Reiki can help an expectant mother in many ways with the miracle of carrying another human inside her and passing on of new life. Using Reiki in the early days of the pregnancy helps reduce exhaustion and nausea. It brings relief to every part of a stretched and aching body at various points up until and including the birth

*The wave lives*
*the life of the wave*
*and at the same time,*
*the life of the water.*
THICH NHAT HANH

Below: What better way to communicate with your baby than to give both of you Reiki. This position is also good to use when you are lying in a warm relaxing bath.

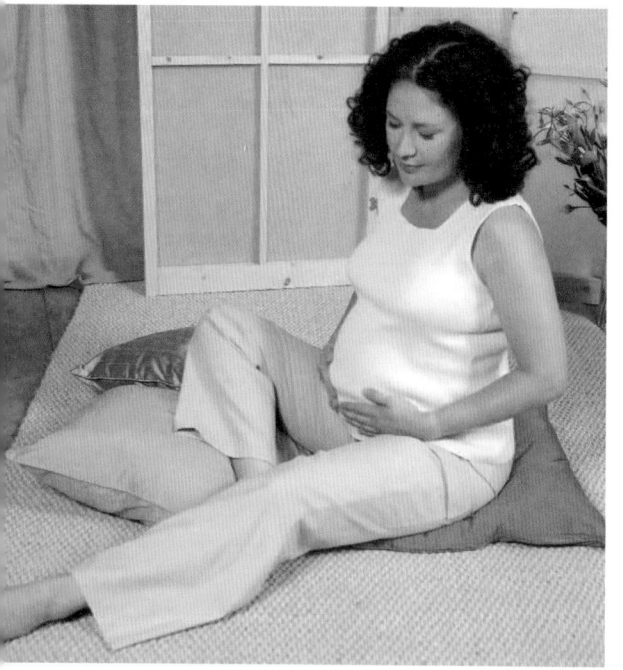

itself. Reiki will help to calm fear of the unknown and will soothe a woman who feels invaded and impatient to give birth. When she is feeling eager to reclaim her own body, Reiki is a gift she can give herself. Reiki can make a baby wriggle with pleasure in the womb, and can also have a calming effect.

## Reiki during birth

You can send Reiki to your baby throughout your pregnancy and during the birth itself, if you or your partner practise. If you don't, get in touch with a Reiki practitioner who will be thrilled to do so. When the time to give birth arrives, Reiki can help to ease the pain to some degree, and help create a loving and peaceful atmosphere for the baby to be born into.

If you have been attuned, you can give your baby Reiki whenever you hold and nurse it. When you feel able, try to give yourself plenty of Reiki at this time, which will help your body to regain its equilibrium and maintain its natural chemical and physiological balance.

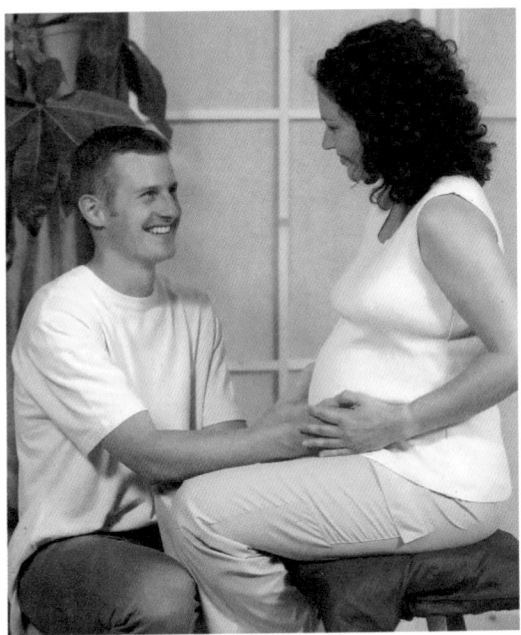

Above: Reiki provides a wonderful way for the expectant partner to bond with baby, and for all three of you to share the experience.

## Some suggested hand positions in pregnancy

- Place one hand on the centre of the sternum and one hand on the back, to treat the back and give healing to the love, or heart, chakra.
- The "spirit level" position is useful in pregnancy for general balance and well-being. Place one hand at the top of the spine/base of neck, and one at the coccyx at the base of the spine.
- Stand behind the recipient and place your hands on her shoulders for a few moments, to help relieve the tension created by carrying the extra weight.
- Treat the feet often, as they take a lot of the strain of a pregnancy..
- In late pregnancy, when the stomach begins to feel heavy, put both hands on either side of the base of the stomach. The mother or her partner may prefer to do this, and as long as the recipient is comfortable it will refresh and support this area.

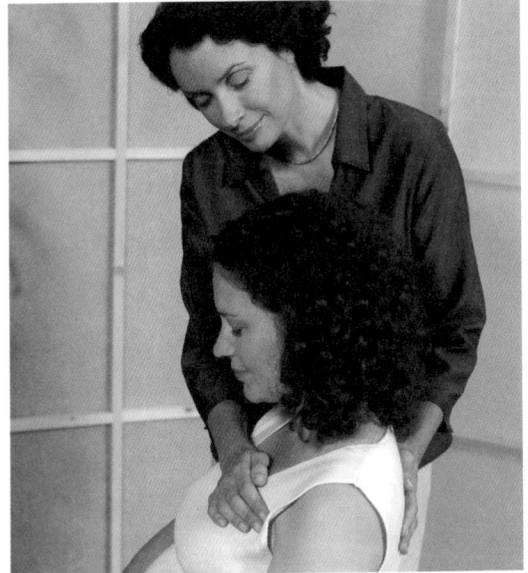

Above: Reiki treatments during pregnancy help to refresh the body and the mind at a time when there is a lot happening.

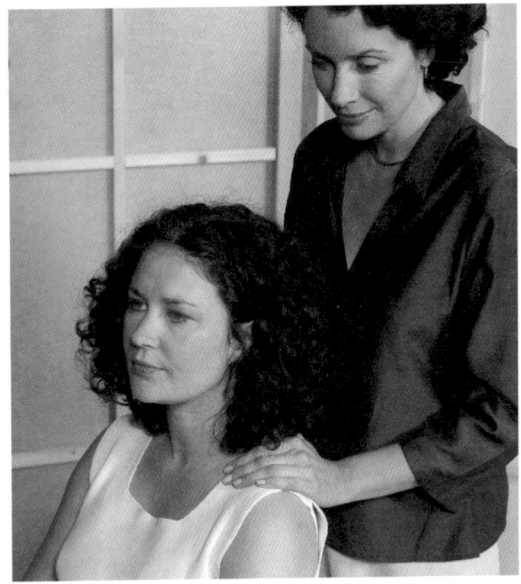

Above: Soothing hands on the shoulders and back can provide great relief from the baby's weight during the final weeks of the pregnancy.

# Reiki for children

People love Reiki at any age, and for youngsters it is fun to experience the sensations of this healing energy while feeling better at the same time. Children take much less time to benefit from Reiki because they are smaller, with faster metabolisms.

Having given Reiki to a nine-year-old with a headache at a party, I found I was a source of entertainment, to be summoned whenever a grazed knee or stomach-ache presented itself, and I began to suspect that fake ailments were being concocted! Parents soon know that Reiki is safe for their children when they see, or in many cases hear about, the positive effects it has.

Reiki sessions with babies and children take much less time than those for adults. Generally, the younger the child, the quicker the Reiki is

Below: Children have great fun feeling the sensations that come from magic Reiki hands.

Above: Children often need no encouragement to try Reiki out on adults and on themselves.

absorbed into the system and the swifter the results. As a guideline, allow ten minutes or less with babies, and about 20–30 minutes with children, but don't worry, you can never do harm with Reiki or overdo it. Children move away or become distracted when they have had enough.

## A treat for parents

Being empowered to help heal your own children, by touch or over distance, must be one of the best feelings in the world. Most youngsters are keen and curious to feel the Reiki once they trust you, but I always ask parents if they would like to be able to do it for their children themselves. They can also give a child the comfort only a parent can bring, especially if they are unwell or feeling miserable. Reiki given to children by their parents creates a subtle bond between them and enriches their understanding of one another. Reiki encourages children and grown-ups to grow, nurtured by the feeling of infinite love, experienced in a tangible, tactile way. A child who knows this love will surely be able to play a part in creating a loving world.

## Children can do reiki too

Sometimes a child will ask, "Do I have to come to you if I want Reiki?" Maybe you will see them one day with their palms flat against themselves, concentrating on whether they can feel the Reiki energy flowing as when you do it. Sometimes, when you are giving Reiki to a parent, a child will want to take part. Children often get sympathetic symptoms if their parents are in distress and they want to be able to help.

The youngest Reiki practitioner I know is Jo, aged 11, who wanted to do Reiki himself after being amazed at his own speedy recovery from hayfever. Two years after his attunement to First

### Some suggested hand positions for treating children

- For a stomach-ache or emotional upset, gently place your hands level on the child's stomach and back while they are standing, or sitting next to you on a sofa.
- For coughs, wheezy colds and hayfever, place your hands level on the child's chest and back. This position is easy to practise when you are both seated on a sofa.
- For a headache, give the child water to drink, and place your hands gently over her or his head.

Remember, children will let you know when Reiki has done the trick. Don't be alarmed if they look flushed after a few minutes – they can get very hot quickly when you are giving them Reiki, on the head or neck in particular.

Degree, he still loves to use Reiki on himself and his family. You must of course always ask the parent's permission before practising Reiki on children and before attuning a youngster into the process.

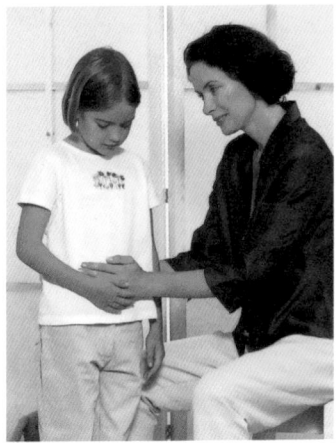

Above: Try these hand positions to ease a stomach-ache.

Above: Any tightness caused by a chest infection or a painful, irritating cough can be eased with this position.

Above: A gentle Reiki touch will ease a child's headache and coax a smile.

# Reiki and the cycle of life

We and every living thing on our planet are connected in a cycle of life, a cosmic web extending through and beyond our own Universe. In birth and death, transformation occurs, forming, changing, continuing.

Sometimes, especially in the Western world, we confuse curing with healing, but they are not the same thing. Though we may have struggled to find the cure for a physical disease, anyone who has been present at a peaceful departure from this world will have witnessed the pervading presence of wholeness, and will know the value of holistic healing at the point of transition. Even as we learn more about the human potential to attain greater longevity in the future, sooner or later we all go with the flow from the river to the ocean. Perhaps subconsciously, we choose to confuse curing and healing to mask our fear of dying, seeing ourselves as losing our loved ones and being lost in a void – isolated, rather than returning to love and life in another state of being. True healing creates a safe space in

Below: The love and light that emanate from a Reiki session remind us that curing a physical illness is not the same as healing the person mentally and spiritually.

## Some suggested hand positions

If someone is in pain, you may prefer to hold your hands over them instead of on the body itself. You can also channel Reiki in shifts, and in other ways such as beaming and distant healing. Use the methods that are most appropriate for you both – Reiki is a gift from our Creator or Creation to all of us and you can never pass it on badly. Wherever the recipient wants to feel the healing power of Reiki will be the right place. Remember how we explored the power of prayer, and how all spiritual disciplines regard prayer as nourishment for the soul, just as food nourishes and sustains the physical body. Even when a person has left their earthly body, you can continue to love and bless them in this way.

- Place both hands on or near the third (solar plexus) chakra, or under the back and on the front of the third chakra. This is the place where we store all our emotions. After, or instead of, placing one hand underneath the recipient, you may like to place one hand on the heart chakra. This will help heal fear and transform it into love.
- Standing at the person's head, visualize drawing the Reiki emotional/mental healing symbol on your palms and in the air above the recipient's head. Then place both your hands under the back of the head, gently rolling it on to one hand and then the other, so that you are both balanced and comfortable. This position is very comforting at any time and facilitates mental healing and peace of mind. If you have not learned how to use the symbols, say a prayer instead.

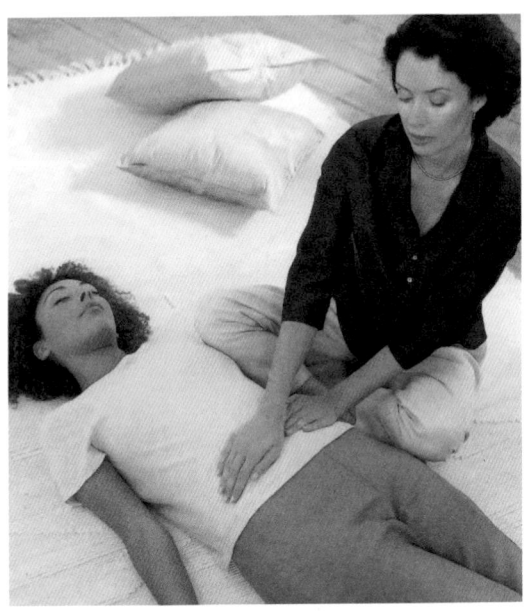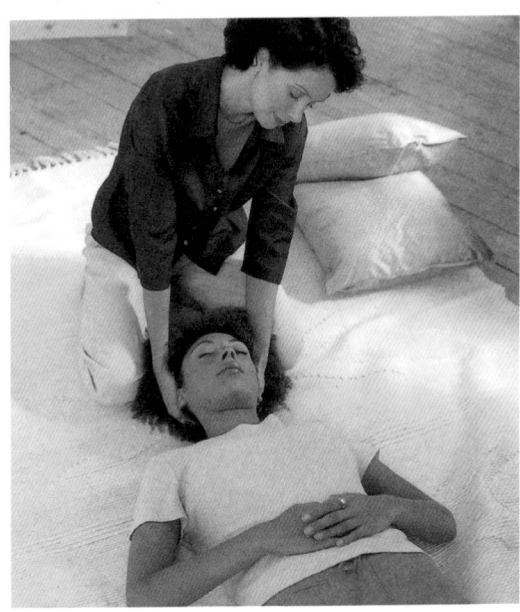

Above and above right: Reiki can relieve pain and anxiety of all kinds whatever the age. Use these caring positions (see details opposite) for people in stressful times, or who are feeling isolated.

which an awareness of unity with the infinite is rekindled. This spiritual reunion, at-oneness with our life-giving Universe, allows a peaceful transition from this world to the next, which is healing in a true sense. Healing allows people to leave this life at peace with themselves, open to transformation without fear or struggle, so that even when an illness is not cured, the person can be healed emotionally and spiritually.

Ancient spiritual teachings and new physics expand our faith and our concepts of finite life but, whatever our beliefs, at the point of death it is possible for us to be without fear. It is negative and disempowering when we feel we cannot do anything about it, and it perpetuates fearfulness. Reiki can help the dying and their loved ones to create a passing-over which is joyful, a surrender to something greater than ourselves, a transformation made without fear and with love.

If someone has been suffering and is afraid, hands-on Reiki from one or more people can be a great comfort in itself. The loving touch

engenders love in the recipient; it facilitates peace and the knowledge that we are all part of the divine plan. For the family and friends it can be a wonderful experience to participate in this healing process, which celebrates life and aids inner peace and therefore swifter recovery from the sense of individual loss. Giving and receiving healing helps us to celebrate the transition of a soul from one place to another, and to sense what is one more natural, joyous progression in the Universe.

During this quiet and reflective time, we see how someone can be happier than ever during the last phases of earthly life. Issues that may have been difficult for the person to live with for years, preventing them from loving themselves and others, may be resolved at last. When we make this emotional transition, our physical bodies can follow with ease. Reiki creates positive change in us at any time, and often gratitude, forgiveness, love and peace are found at this most special and sacred stage of life.

# Reiki for animals

Animals enjoy receiving Reiki just as much as we do. A great many people feel the healing power of animals through their pets, which express love unconditionally and often comfort us when we are fearful.

No matter how great or small, all creatures yield to healing hands. It is a wonderful experience to share Reiki with the animal kingdom, strengthening and reminding us of our connection to all life.

## Treating animals

All animals can be treated with Reiki as a tonic or to ease suffering. I have tried it with beetles and dogs, and it works. With a pet, you can place your hands on or over an injury or wound, and you will generally know when it has had enough. It will move away, become distracted, or begin to preen or wash itself. With an energetic pet, it may be more successful to send distant healing, perhaps programmed for every alternate hour

during the night while it sleeps. The results can be seen the following day, and this technique would be suitable for a hamster or other nocturnal animal.

Small animals, such as weak or injured birds found in the garden, will benefit from being held in Reiki hands for ten minutes, which will probably be enough. Reiki is also very beneficial to animals who are emotionally upset.

The Reiki treatment for your pet will swiftly and safely reach wherever it is required, so it is always beneficial. You can also complement your hands-on healing with a distant healing, sent to the local stable or veterinary surgery for example, but don't send Reiki while the animal is under general anaesthetic.

Below: Cats are particularly sensitive to touch and will show their pleasure when you are giving them affection. When you use Reiki hands, they will enjoy it even more.

Below: Cupping the head of your pet calmly and carefully between Reiki hands will send a soothing yet powerful healing energy. You don't need to apply any pressure.

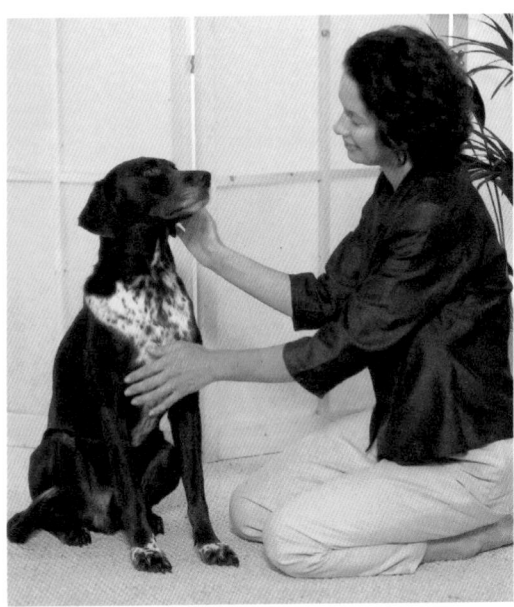

Above: You can give pets a daily Reiki treatment, helping to maintain their general health and happiness. Spend a few moments calming and settling your pet.

Above: Gentle and calm hand positions will reassure your pet. Specific problems can be helped quickly and easily by placing your hands directly on the affected limb.

Left: If it is difficult to know exactly where the discomfort is, or you are just maintaining health, simply place your hands where it is comfortable for you and your pet, and let Reiki do the rest instinctively.

## Some suggested hand positions for treating animals

The following positions are for pet-sized creatures, so adapt as necessary.

- Hold your hands either side of the ribcage, with the animal seated on your lap or on the floor. This will treat the whole body and the Reiki will reach central parts immediately.
- Put one hand on the head of your pet as though you are going to stroke its ears, and one very lightly on the middle of its back.
- Hold the animal in your hands, with one hand at the top of the spine and one by its tail at the base of the spine.

# Reiki and healing plants

Reiki extends to all the natural world. It can even be used to encourage healthy plants both in the home and the garden. You can treat the plants directly or give their food and water a Reiki blessing.

Those who have hugged trees will often have experienced a strong healing sensation. This can be channelled at a smaller scale to the plants in your own house and garden; Reiki is reciprocated in all Nature.

## Reiki for houseplants

There is no substitute for light and water, but plants love Reiki. There are many ways in which you can give them a Reiki treat. Houseplants are living in an unnatural environment and will appreciate the healing touch of Reiki as it offers them some natural, universal healing. Put Reiki hands directly on to the leaves, or the stems of a large houseplant. For smaller plants, cup the pot in your hand. Another way to give plants Reiki is to give it to the water you are going to use to water them with, and in the same way you can

Above: The very water you give your plants, if imbued with Reiki, can provide nourishment taken from your hands.

Left: You can give Reiki to the compost or plant food as well as in the water, to ensure the plant roots receive healing. Create a special area in the patio or garden room where you can sit and relax and simply enjoy being amongst Nature.

give Reiki to fertilizers, compost or plant food. It is thought that plants respond to human touch and the human voice, so increase the power of your treatment by talking to your plants too.

## Reiki in the garden

As well as using Reiki to enhance your houseplants, you can also help your garden by filling it with Reiki energy. Before you plant bulbs or seedlings, hold them in the palms of your hands for ten minutes to fortify and bless them. Draw the power symbol in the soil after planting them carefully. When pruning, hold the cut branch in Reiki hands for a few moments.

In areas of your garden where you spend time relaxing, hang a little drawing or terracotta model of an appropriate Reiki symbol to gain the soothing or energizing effects of your garden. As you walk around, give your plants a Reiki brush with your fingertips as you pass them by. And as you sit enjoying your thriving garden in the fresh air, send Reiki by drawing the distant healing and power symbols in the air, or beam to the whole garden, visualizing a golden-white light around each plant.

### Some suggested hand positions for treating plants

- Sit at a table and put a houseplant in front of you, placing your hands around the base of the pot. This will treat the plant roots and encourage strong growth. Move your hands progressively up the pot if you like.
- Draw the Reiki power symbol in the soil around the plant with a pencil or your finger.
- Hold your hands over the flowers of a plant in Reiki fashion and see if you can feel the energy. Plants have auras, too, and while you are giving them Reiki you can open up to seeing them. Look at the space about 2.5 cm (1 in) around the edges of the plant, and let your eyes become unfocused. With practice, you will see white feathery fronds which merge into a colour, and this is the plant's energy field or aura. Try sending healing across the room and note the vibrancy.
- Fill a bottle with water and give it hands-on Reiki just as you would your own food and drink. Use it for watering plants. Cut flowers will last longer in a vase of Reiki water.

Above: Cup your hands around bulbs before you plant them, perhaps empowered with a Reiki symbol in the soil.

Right: The plants in your garden will benefit from being brushed by Reiki fingertips as you walk past.

# Reiki and Other Therapies

*One moon shows in every pool*
*In every pool the one moon.*

A ZEN SAYING

# Flower essences and aromatherapy

Aromatherapy oils and floral essences offer wonderful benefits on their own, but there are some very effective ways to complement these beautiful plant therapies with Reiki. The most obvious of these is to Reiki your flower essences and oils simply by holding them in your hands – a great way of giving yourself two treatments in one.

Aromatherapy massages are a heavenly experience, but if you are using lavender oil to counteract stress, for instance, the effects can be enhanced by drawing the healing symbol in the air above the recipient, as you might during a regular Reiki treatment. In the same way, one can complement the healing of emotional issues by using Reiki with flower essences. Each essence has a special benefit or "life lesson" encapsulated within. Observing the nature of these remedies can be a marvellous and speedy way to articulate a confusing emotional issue.

Above: If you are making your own flower infusions, hold the bowl in your hands for a few minutes so that Reiki will impart its additional benefits.

Below: Essential oils are the scented active compounds of plants extracted in a highly concentrated form.

## Using Reiki with flowers

The essences of plants can have a profound effect. When you are giving someone a massage with aromatherapy oils, it is a natural part of the process to treat your recipient to some Reiki as you touch them. In this way, you will be charging the oils with Reiki and lengthening the healing effects of the oils themselves. You can also send Reiki to a treatment, or to your oils before a session. Draw Reiki symbols on or in them if you like.

Rescue Remedy, a powerful Bach flower essence, along with other flower remedies, work beautifully with Reiki, as they are strong and subtle healers. When you are using flower remedies, you can hold the bottles in Reiki hands or send Reiki as you take the essence.

Right: The simplest way of complementing your flower essences is to hold your hands above the bottles in a Reiki blessing.

Above: Giving Reiki to a bowl of essential oil before giving a massage is a powerful combination of two therapies.

Right: Gently rub the Reikied oil into your temples as part of a complementary self-treatment.

# Reiki with colour

There is great scope within Reiki for complementary healing with colour. This can be effectively carried out during hands-on or distant-sending Reiki sessions. Visualizing or sending colours is beneficial for the recipient of Reiki, not least because he or she can actively participate, and can continue to do so at home.

Those who ask to receive Reiki are creating their own healing, but whereas we are dependent on a practitioner for Reiki, the healing benefits of colour and positive imagination are bestowed on us from an early age.

People who can see the aura, or energetic field, around living things know that we are truly colourful characters. Our many aspects create energy which vibrates at a certain rate, creating colour in and around our bodies. During the 19th century the Russian electrical engineer Semyon Kirlian discovered how to photograph the energy field, and there are now many Kirlian photographers who can give you a print of your chromatic make-up as it is today. Many people can read auras, seeing the colours surrounding us as representing our state of health on all levels. This can be helpful in locating the cause of disharmony and disease.

Above: Learning about colour can increase our insight into healing the self and others. Blue is the colour of healing in Reiki.

## Reiki and colour

| chakra | colour |
| --- | --- |
| root | red |
| sacral | orange |
| solar plexus | yellow |
| heart | green/pink |
| throat | blue |
| pineal | indigo |
| crown | violet/purple |

Left: Soak some blue stones in a bowl of water, then drink the water. For added effect give the stones and the bowl some Reiki first.

### Reiki and colour harmony

- If you are feeling blue, send pink. Enjoy a Reiki self-treat, visualizing pale pink if you are feeling sad, or green if you are irritated or angry. Remember that you can send Reiki to anything, even a visualization. Sometimes, the colour you need is difficult to visualize, so look at a patch of it, consciously soaking it up.

- Literally drink in the healing powers of a colour by leaving spring water in a glass container of your chosen colour. The effects of this "hydrochromatic therapy" is increased if you stand the container in the sunshine for a few hours, or place Reiki hands on the bottle or tumbler. Always sip slowly and gently, and use with caution.

- Paint light bulbs different colours and use them in your own Reiki treatments and for others. Paint each one the colour of a chakra, and keep them available for a lamp in your healing space. Taking 10–15 minutes for each chakra, the colour and the Reiki will balance and restore harmony in the whole person.

- Stand a few feet away from the recipient, holding your palms out straight, and visualize him or her surrounded by gold while you send Reiki. You can also visualize a gold shroud at the beginning and end of a hands-on Reiki session.

- Do this for fun with a friend. "Beam" a colour in the same way as above with your arms out straight, then try and guess which colour is being visualized. You can both finish with white or gold to heal and protect. You can also give this to yourself before a recipient arrives: surround yourself in gold or imagine a pink bubble around yourself to create a positive and loving space between you.

## Colourful creation

Colour is such a beautifully simple thing to use in healing, making the most of light in all its myriad forms by absorbing it into our beings. This can be done in a number of ways – how many times have you gazed at a colour, breathing and drinking it in as though you could look at it for hours? We are all responsive to colour, instinctively preferring one to another on different days and surrounding ourselves with colours we can live with harmoniously.

The beneficial effects of colours in the treatment of certain conditions is well documented and the chart to the left illustrates the colours which correspond to each chakra in the body. Always consult a qualified colour therapist with a specific problem. Next time you have a sore throat, wrap something blue around your neck; the blue light will help to balance and restore your throat chakra and the surrounding parts. You can give it some Reiki as well before you put it on. Red, worn or seen, can lift depression and help to motivate. Each colour has its own energy; the colour spectrum is called the "rainbow bridge", linking our planet to higher worlds.

Right: Bring more colour into your life, in your home and your wardrobe, and benefit from its vibrancy and energy-enhancing qualities.

# Reki with reflexology

Reiki is so inclusive in its nature that it complements other healing arts, especially tactile ones where the benefit of the energy channelled through the hands is at once relaxing and invigorating. Reflexology is a natural fit for reiki healing.

Reflexology, the practice of treating the whole body by touching the feet and sometimes the palms, is an especially valuable example of a therapy which complements Reiki successfully.

Reflexology was known to ancient civilizations in India and other regions, and is now acknowledged all over the world as a respected, effective and enjoyable form of healing. These days, many qualified reflexologists use Reiki in conjunction with their own methods, and if you practise Reiki you can give yourself a Reiki reflexology full-body treat by holding your hands on or over the pressure points of the foot.

Every part of the foot is represented by an organ in the physical body. For example, by holding the inside edges of one or both feet, you are in fact applying Reiki to the spine. (This is especially useful for a self-treatment in a comfortable position.) By placing your hands on the outside edge of one or both feet, you are applying Reiki to every joint on the edge of your body, travelling downwards from shoulder, elbow and hip to the knee and ankle on either side. Pressure points for the various organs are

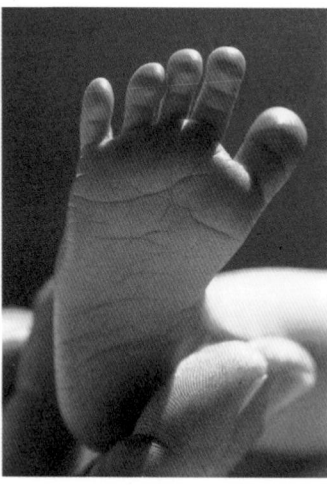

Above: The feet and the hands are maps of our entire systems, from the very first days of our existence.

Left: Giving your feet gentle Reiki will give the whole body a tonic.

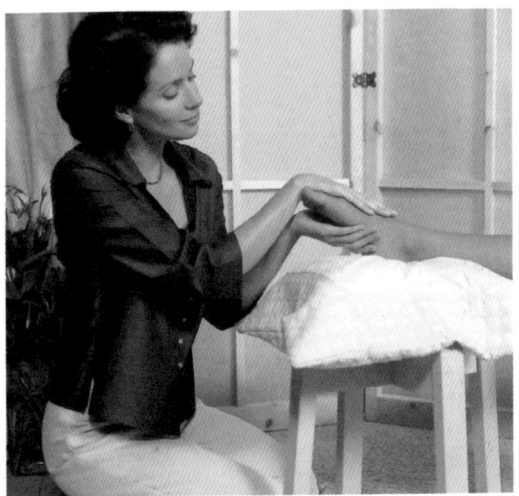

Above: Hold the feet of the recipient in cupped hands for just five minutes. This is an effective position for someone who needs a gentle Reiki session.

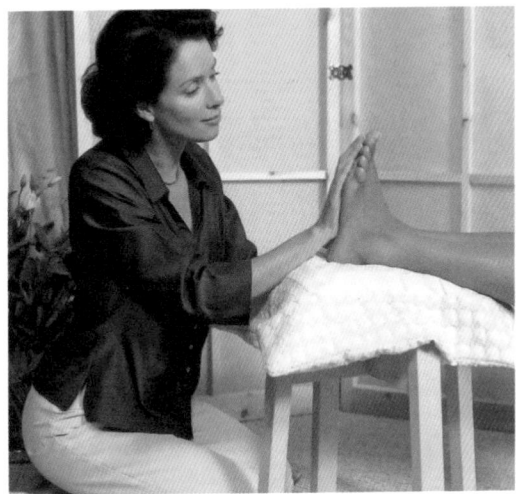

Above: At the end of the session, return your recipient to earth with a grounding palm-to-foot experience to connect and refresh.

fairly close together on the foot, so you may have trouble differentiating which area of the body you are treating with Reiki. However, this can only be a benefit, as Reiki energy knows exactly where to go, and you cannot overdo it. Some reflexologists use their thumbs to channel Reiki, as this is how they generally hold or massage a pressure point when giving a treatment.

In some instances of serious injury or illness, the body part in need of relief cannot be reached. By holding the feet in Reiki mode, you can overcome this difficulty and still be in contact with the location on the body. Using reflexology and Reiki on the feet is a very gentle therapy for the body, and can be as helpful as a hands-on full-body Reiki session.

Giving Reiki to your feet is also of benefit to the feet themselves. We often disregard blisters, calluses and other painful complaints because we don't have the time to put our feet up for long and repair the damage. Enjoying foot Reiki will benefit your body and put a spring in your step.

*It is in your hands*
*to create a better*
*world for all who*
*live in it.*
NELSON MANDELA

### Origins of reflexology

Treatment of pressure points on the feet and hands has been practised for thousands of years, the earliest known evidence being a relief in a mastaba (funerary monument) at Saqqara in Egypt, dated around 2,500–2,300 BCE. In ancient China, the feet were worked in conjunction with acupuncture, and were treated first to stimulate the whole body and find areas of disturbance. Foot treatment was also practised in India and Indonesia and among Native American Indians.

# Reiki and crystal healing

Crystals and stones have benign powers of their own. Their transformational and healing qualities have been well-known to people of many ancient cultures, and we are now rediscovering them, just as Reiki and other healing gifts have returned to us.

These powerhouses of the planet heal with no help from us, yet they can be programmed with positive wishes and healing intent. Each gem or stone has a distinct healing function and energy vibration, which is both profound and subtle, and benefits all living things. The vibrational essence of a gem or precious stone has the power to heal at the very source of an illness before the symptoms manifest in the physical body.

## Magic in multiplicity

Just as crystals are multi-faceted, their powers to heal are also varied and versatile. Colour and structure are both significant elements in their potency to help everything from backache to psychic development. When we hold a

Above: Infusing crystals with Reiki will enrich their own qualities and energize a room or crystal grid.

### Experimenting with crystals

Notice the marvellous effects of crystals in many aspects of day-to-day life. Experiment with crystals to feel their own power, then charge them with Reiki and observe any changes. You can become intimate with both your crystals and Reiki in this way.

- Cleanse your crystals every now and then by holding them under running water or burying them in sea salt for a few hours.
- Place a clean crystal in your water filter so that you can absorb its healing power when you drink the water. You can charge it with Reiki too, or even send Reiki to your crystal(s).
- Give some Reiki to a crystal and place it in your bath.
- Place crystals on a windowsill late at night so that the first, life-giving rays of the morning sun will cleanse them and nurture their strength.

- When the moon is waning, and especially when it is new, it will bathe and cleanse a crystal placed on a windowsill; when it is waxing or full, it will increase its power. Rose quartz is often used for emotional healing and the moon is associated with our psyches and emotions, so this stone may be particularly responsive to lunar cycles. You can note the astrological sign the moon is passing through, and use a crystal with relevant properties.
- Give a crystal some Reiki and place it in a plant pot or hang it above flowers. Place it in your food cupboard to promote long and healthy life.
- Place a small amethyst on your sixth, "third eye", chakra while you are lying down during a self-treatment. Amethysts are highly regarded by crystal healers as they have special properties which encourage insight and spiritual transformation.

crystal or stone on or over a part of the body or in our hand while sending Reiki, it focuses and amplifies our healing wishes. Held on our own bodies, they likewise heal and strengthen, balancing energy within us and promoting positivity, not unlike the way Reiki symbols work.

## The history of using crystals

Discoveries of crystal skulls at sites around the world and the technology that gemstones have given the human race today have increased our understanding of crystals and their ability to send, transform and absorb information. In ancient Sumeria, Arab scholars were adept in the arts of astronomy, astrology and alchemy, combining this expertise with their use of gifts from the earth for healing. The qualities contained in the essence of a gemstone were often taken into the body in the form of a gem elixir, drinking water which had had a crystal or stone soaking in it for a day or more.

In Indian and Western astrology, birthstones can be sources of power in a particular aspect of a horoscope, and traditional astrologers place great importance on the appropriate energy of

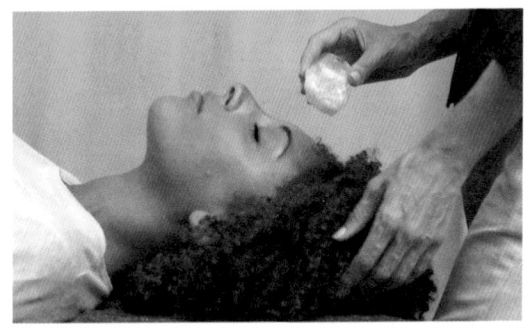

Above: Hold a quartz crystal which has been charged with Reiki above the recipient's head to focus healing.

a crystal for an individual. Some people believe it is unlucky to buy your own crystal, and this is probably to ensure it is given in love. These days, we are getting better at giving ourselves love and many people use their intuition, simply holding a crystal and choosing the one which feels best in their hands. If you have never taken much notice of crystals, spend some time holding them and see how you feel. Live with them for a few days and you will appreciate how unique each one is. It is good to share your responses to different stones with others.

Above: Holding a quartz crystal on your forehead during meditation or self-treatments can enhance perception and intuition.

Above: Hold a crystal near your heart when making an affirmation.

Above: Place crystals in your palms to feel a powerful circuit of energy while sending Reiki.

# Reiki and affirmations

Reiki is a catalyst for growth and positivity in all areas of life, a message from a loving Universe, bringing with it a realization that we are responsible for ourselves and our own healing. It shares with us the revelation that we create our own reality.

Our thoughts are forms of energy, just like everything else; people who can see auras say that anger, for example, manifests itself as a red, spiky movement around the body. Technology now enables us to photograph and measure the energy fields our bodies emanate – the visible results of our emotions.

Practising Reiki for oneself can be described as a healing affirmation on its own, as we are demonstrating that we are worth spending time on. Making time for others comes more easily to many of us, as we are raised to look after other people first, and we can see an hour a day spent on ourselves as indulgent if we are busy. Reiki allows us to feel and recognize ourselves as part of something greater, each of us an expression

Above: Speaking your affirmations to yourself is an interesting way to discover more about yourself. Use a mirror for maximum effect.

Below: An affirmation can be a wish to banish a negative or bad habit; you could write it down and burn it away.

of the Divine. An affirmation is a positive statement, and a positive statement made to oneself is swiftly followed by an echo from the Universe, which dislikes an empty space. When we begin each morning feeling thankful and happy with life, we are expecting our lives to be good and full, and the Universe responds, likewise. If we wake up fearful of what the day will bring and feeling desperate, the Universe will respond similarly, making us feel weighed down. What was once dismissed as "all in the mind" is now valued for the same reason.

There is no better time to try out this "attitude of gratitude" than when you are feeling dreadful. This is not because we are seeking sainthood, but because it is really efffective at turning a "bad" situation into one of value. Don't hang on to it, take a leap of faith, with as much of an open mind as you can muster, and say, "My life is good

## Using affirmations

Reiki can be sent to any affirmation because it is a creative and positive use of our emotions. "I dedicate this healing to the highest good." "I release the need to smoke or use drugs." "I am motivated by love. I communicate with clarity."

Sometimes we are mystified by the cause of an illness or emotional upset. We are helpless because our brains are vexed. Remember that intent is everything, and by standing back from the situation in our minds it is easier to say something helpful, such as: "I thank my body and the Universe for showing me there is conflict to resolve. I understand and release the belief system which causes this condition.

When you begin a self-treat, send some Reiki to your affirmation of the moment. Or, give your Reiki recipient a few moments to think of an appropriate goal they would like to achieve.

and all is well, and things are getting even better and we are growing from here." An important thing to remember about affirmations is to Keep Them Positive. Words like "don't", "can't" and "won't" can be less effective and confusing. Make your affirmation in the present tense. Decide on a positive sentence that is comfortable to you and "feel" it as much as you can while you say it, seeing a positive situation or your smiling self.

Affirmations connect us to our universe by showing us we can create our own reality in the very ways we want to.

Saying an affirmation aloud and with feeling will endow it with more energy, and so will looking into your own eyes in a mirror. Tapping (not rubbing) the thymus gland in the centre of your chest while speaking an affirmation will also empower you. Words spoken with intent are what your body and the Universe need to hear, and gratitude and trust in life will in turn attract more to be grateful for.

Below: Writing affirmations down on a piece of paper and then giving hands-on Reiki to the written wish is also effective.

Below: For even greater effect, strengthen your written wishes with a symbol and place the paper under your pillow before you go to bed.

# Reiki and meditations

Meditation is used by people of every culture and religion, and is a powerful tool which enhances our health in every way. All you need to begin benefitting from meditation is 15 free minutes each day. If you begin your day in this way you soon find your mind is clearer and calmer, and your body more relaxed and easy.

Far from spacing you out, meditation promotes "less haste, more speed" as efficiency increases with mental awareness. Meditating on your own breath or on a positive visualization causes the heart rate to fall, and the immune system to rise by 50 per cent.

Buddhists detach from all but the constant breath in meditation and realize unity with the Universe through chanting mantras, as spiritual affirmations. By doing this they transcend an attachment to suffering in life. The Sufis, mystic Muslims, are famous for their whirling meditations, where one hand is held above the head in a meditation of motion in which they connect with One, Allah. They realize the connection between human and divine, and "die before they die", realizing the impermanence

Above: Meditating on clarity and love before a Reiki session allows you to be in the present moment.

Below: Being aware of your breathing rhythms releases finite time and space.

of earthly life through an experience of the infinite. Hindus contemplate the wheel of life, ever-changing, and Christian gnostics unite in the mystery of creation through meditation. Meditating on something or nothing brings increased health and awareness.

### Reiki, music and meditation

| chakra | musical note | mantra |
|---|---|---|
| root | C | lam |
| sacral | D | vam |
| solar plexus | E | ram |
| heart | F | yam |
| throat | G | ham |
| pineal | A | ksham |
| crown | B | om |

Above: Tapping the thymus gland is a way of absorbing new chosen belief systems.

Above: Meditation influences all aspects of your life and is effective in increasing levels of creativity and imagination.

### All in the breath

- Try this fascinating exercise and discover how much your breath affects your everyday senses. Stand before a plant and look at it for a few seconds, then close your eyes. Take a deep breath, filling your body with oxygen and feeling it reach up to your shoulders as you breathe in. Breathe some more, so that your breaths become natural and relaxed, and be conscious of breathing from the centre of your being. During an inward breath, open your eyes and look at the plant, observing what you see. Repeat, this time opening your eyes as you breathe out. What differences do you notice, however subtle? A friend told me that he had done this in front of a fir tree in the Spanish mountains – the tree looked sharper and aggressive with an intake of breath and gentler while exhaling. This exercise has its origins in Taoism, the practice of breathing and living with the Tao, the Way or natural flow of life.

- Sit comfortably, and place your hands on your heart chakra or in your lap. Breathe comfortably, eyes closed, and focus on any one of the four Reiki symbols. You could meditate on the emotional/mental healing symbol for inner peace. Visualize the symbol before you, feeling its energy and contemplating its name and meaning. Meditation on Reiki symbols will encourage creative insight as well as increased awareness. You can also do this with all four symbols, beginning with the master symbol and ending with the power symbol.

- Connect with the core of yourself, seeing it as a golden-white light in your centre. Slowly, expand the light inside you until it extends to the tips of your fingers and toes. Be aware of your light overflowing into the room then the building and gradually outward to the whole universe, before bringing it home to your being again.

# Index

Published by Lorenz Books
an imprint of Anness Publishing Limited
www.annesspublishing.com
info@anness.com

A CIP catalogue record is available from the
British Library

Publisher: Joanna Lorenz
Senior editor: Joanne Rippin
Designer: Nigel Partridge
Special photography: Fiona Pragoff
Production controller: Ben Worley

With thanks to the other photographers and picture libraries for
additional images.

## AUTHOR'S NOTE

The following people have given love and help with the creation of
this book, and I thank them for their generosity and wisdom – Richard
Wheeler, John Watson, Sally Hamilton, Jon Heasman, Kate Musselwhite,
Caz Waters, Sarah Mason, Hiro Arai, Debs Grinstead, Kevin Acton, Rachel
and Alice Jones, Maggie, Paul and Eduardo Fernandez, and Rowena
Williams and Bashar. Love and happiness to all.

## PUBLISHER'S NOTE

The reader should not regard the recommendations, ideas and techniques
expressed and described in this book as substitutes for the advice of a
qualified medical practitioner or other qualified professional. Any use
to which the recommendations, ideas and techniques are put is at the
reader's sole discretion and risk.

## ABOUT THE AUTHOR

Carmen Fernandez is a practising Reiki master and has felt the power
of Reiki affect every aspect of her life. Carmen is a strong believer in the
healing power of universal love and the astonishing results that can be
achieved through the channelling of natural energy, and has shared her
knowledge and expertise in this book.